PIETRO ARCHIATI worked as a missionary in Laos (during the Vietnam war), New York and South Africa. When he discovered Anthroposophy in 1977, it soon became the passion of his life. Pietro is a popular speaker, working internationally, and has written several books, including *From Christianity to Christ, Reincarnation in Modern Life* and *The Great Religions*. With his colleague Monika Grimm, he also publishes key texts by Rudolf Steiner in the original German.

SPIRITUAL SCIENCE IN THE THIRD MILLENNIUM

Intellectuality Versus Anthroposophy

Pietro Archiati

TEMPLE LODGE

Temple Lodge Publishing Ltd.
Hillside House, The Square
Forest Row, RH18 5ES

www.templelodge.com

First published in English by Temple Lodge Publishing 2015

Originally published in German under the title *Geisteswissenschaft im 3. Jahrtausend* by Rudolf Steiner Ausgaben 2014. This translation is based on the 5th edition of January 2015, retitled *Der Intellektualismus und die Anthroposophie*

Translated by Pauline Wehrle with thanks to Paul V. O'Leary and the author for additional editing

A CIP catalogue record for this book is available from the British Library

ISBN 978 1 906999 78 0

Author photo by Foto de Santis
Cover by Morgan Creative
Typeset by DP Photosetting, Neath, West Glamorgan
Printed and bound by 4Edge Ltd., Essex

Contents

Preface
1

1 Is There Such a Thing as Spiritual Science?
Christian Clement's Introduction to his 'Critical Edition' of Rudolf Steiner's Fundamental Texts
7

2 Are Faith and Spirit Merely a Private Concern?
An Attempt to Shelve Spiritual Science
27

3 Does Anthroposophy Have a Future?
Intellectuality and Human Beings in Search of Spirit
45

Postscript
65

Notes
77

Select Bibliography
Works by Rudolf Steiner in English Translation
87

Preface

Christian Clement, an Associate Professor at the Brigham Young University (in Provo, Utah, USA), made his appearance in 2013 as an editor of works by Rudolf Steiner.* In his Introduction to the first volume (Volume 5 in a series of 8 volumes) he wrote down his thoughts about Rudolf Steiner's spiritual science. He presents spiritual science as a kind of 'theory', one among many, as a product of the general way we 'imagine things to be'. Thus, he describes Rudolf Steiner as someone who repeatedly changes his mind, from book to book, from one edition to the next—someone who 'clearly carries out a revision of his earlier concept of the spirit' (Introduction, p. lxii), and undertakes 'a shift in the evaluation of the role of Christianity' (p. lxx).

Anthroposophy can certainly not have suddenly arisen as an integrated whole, without having passed through an evolution. Everybody is evolving, including Rudolf Steiner. But that does not mean that a metamorphosis or a new formation has to be a 'revision' or a correction of what was said earlier—which is then proved to have been wrong. When, in the case of a flower, the coloured blossom appears, this does not come as a correction of a faulty green leaf. It is, on the contrary, a further metamorphosis of the plant, which, without the existence of the green leaf, would not have been able to arise. Rudolf Steiner was always comparing the arising of his spiritual science with the evolution of a *living organism*.

Genuine 'revisions', however, can certainly occur in struggling to find the way to present things. When it is a matter of assessing what form of expression would be suitable for this or that audience or readership, mistaken choices cannot always be

*See *Schriften – Kritische Ausgabe (SKA), Band 5: Schriften über Mystik, Mysterienwesen und Religionsgeschichte*, Frommann-Holzboog/Rudolf Steiner Verlag, 2013. (Ed.)

avoided. Nobody can know in advance what other people will find acceptable, also not Rudolf Steiner. But the manner of presenting something is a superficial aspect of it. It is similar to the way the soil influences a plant. It may not be much of a hindrance or it may be a great one, but it will not make the slightest difference to the forces of growth.

What Clement writes in his Introduction to volume 5 reminds one of the conversation between Goethe and Schiller, where Goethe tries to explain the archetypal phenomenon of plants. Influenced by the intellectuality of Kant, Schiller cannot 'experience' the spiritual reality that Goethe sees at work in plants. What he sees is, for Schiller, an abstract idea that has no reality. Goethe writes:

> [. . .] the old resentment wanted to assert itself; but I pulled myself together and replied: 'I can be very happy about the fact that I have ideas without knowing it, and even see them with my eyes.'[1]

The particulars of anthroposophically orientated spiritual science, which Rudolf Steiner brought as a unique gift to humanity's evolution of consciousness, can be summarized in the following statements:

1. There is a spiritual world, which contains the first causes of all that happens in the visible world. Human beings can get to know this world just as objectively and scientifically as they can know the physical world.
2. To obtain this knowledge, our thinking has to be further developed to the extent that it becomes free of the body, and through 'Imagination', 'Inspiration' and 'Intuition' develops an essentially new way of functioning.
3. Rudolf Steiner is the first, and until today the only, human being who has developed thinking in this way. In doing this he has created a science of the spirit that extends in all directions, and nothing in humanity can be compared to this.

Christian Clement does not go into these particular aspects of Rudolf Steiner's spiritual science. But going into it in detail is essential if one is to deal with anthroposophy scientifically. The present book argues against the scientific nature of Clement's work, in so far as he considers the following to be 'indisputable':

> Anthroposophy as a world conception is indisputably a child of the connection of German idealism with German mysticism within Rudolf Steiner's thinking; whether the child is conceived legitimately or illegitimately is not under consideration here. (Introduction, p. xlii)

Anthroposophy is said to have arisen out of the marriage between idealism and mysticism in the same way that a child is born from a mother and father. A spiritual event—the birth of anthroposophy—is being compared with a natural event, the birth of a child. The decisive question here, as to whether Clement means that *everything* in the child can be explained as coming from what is found in the parents, remains unanswered. If the child brings into the world something new that isn't found in the parents, then everything might be found in it that is in its parents—but the individual aspects, what is special to the child, is not touched upon or explained.

When comparing animals and man, natural science looks at what they have in common, and sees man as a more advanced animal. The point here, too, is that even if everything that is in the animal is also in man in a metamorphosed form the decisive question as to whether man, *over and above that*, shows significant features that are *lacking* in the animal is not even asked. Here, looking at the similarities, at what is comparable, does not help. It is similar when comparing anthroposophy with idealism and mysticism. We can be erudite enough to find in anthroposophy everything that is in idealism and mysticism. But this does not answer the question of whether anthroposophy contains anything *beyond this*, some essential ingredient that exists neither in idealism or mysticism. The present book attempts to prove that this essential ingredient exists, and that an *objectively scientific knowledge of the spiritual world* is acquired by way of a further development of thinking, to the point of a new kind of activity that is not mentioned at all in either idealism or mysticism.

In the year 1925, shortly before his death, Rudolf Steiner wrote in his final foreward to his *Occult Science, An Outline* a detailed account of the originality and uniqueness of his spiritual science. This description at the same time makes it clear that modern intellectuality is bound to misunderstand anthroposophy:

> The content of what is seen spiritually can only be reproduced in pictures (imaginations) through which inspirations speak that come from intuitively experienced spiritual beings. [...]
>
> I am fully aware that my knowledge of spiritual matters is the result of my own vision. [...] Just as a mathematician goes from one thought to another, without anything unconscious, autosuggestion, etc., playing a part in them, I told myself that spiritual vision must go in the same way from one objective imagination to another, without anything else living in the soul than the spiritual content of a clear, lucid consciousness. [...]
>
> This is how I perceived the results of my vision. They were to begin with 'perceptions' that lived without names.
>
> In order to share them, I needed words to describe them. It was only *afterwards* that I looked in old descriptions of spiritual matters, so as to be able to express in words what was at first wordless. I used these descriptive words freely, so that hardly *a single* word I used coincided with what it meant where I found it.
>
> But my search for the possibility of expressing myself only happened *after* the content had arisen in my own vision.
>
> Out of the nature of my own researching vision, I knew how to shut out *what I had previously read.*
>
> People then found in my expressions echoes of old presentations. Without going into their meaning, they got stuck in the form of expression. If I spoke of 'lotus flowers' in the human astral body, that proved to them that I was reproducing Indian ideas where one finds such expressions. If I spoke of 'astral body' this was for them a result of reading documents from the Middle Ages. If I used the term angeloi, archangeloi, etc., I was simply warming up the ideas of Christian gnosis.
>
> This kind of thinking, which merely touched the surface of the

matter, was constantly being held against me. (GA 13, pp. 26–31. *Occult Science – An Outline*)

This book is intended to be an introduction to anthroposophy by contrasting it with modern intellectuality. In Christian Clement's work intellectuality shows its inability to grasp Rudolf Steiner's spiritual science, which is based on a further development of thinking, through which human beings acquire the capacity to know the world of spirit in an objective and scientific way. Such a spiritual science can give human beings the power to overcome the destructive effect of an intellectualism that does not recognize the spirit, either in nature or in human beings.

1
Is There Such a Thing as Spiritual Science?
Christian Clement's Introduction to his 'Critical Edition' of Rudolf Steiner's Fundamental Texts

In what follows I shall try to analyse a few of the important thoughts in Christian Clement's Introduction to Volume 5 of his *Works on Mysticism, the Nature of the Mysteries and the History of Religions* in the SKA (*Schriften – Kritische Ausgabe*) series about Rudolf Steiner's works, primarily from the point of view of the spirit that breathes within them. The spirit of modern scientific methods that Clement claims for himself requires strict objectivity in dealing with the object of research. I have endeavoured to proceed in such a way that nothing of what Clement has written is missing that is necessary to comprehend my discussions.

In his Introduction to Rudolf Steiner's books on Mysticism and Christianity,[2] Clement speaks about 'The sketchy outline of the form anthroposophy assumed later on' (p. xxxix). In these books, Rudolf Steiner tries to prove the truth of the 'method [...] of anthroposophical research [...] namely the further development of the phenomenological/morphological method of Goethe's by applying these to the spheres of the soul and the spirit.' (pp. xxix–xxx) Clement explains further:

> Just as Goethe had endeavoured to do [...] Rudolf Steiner tried to trace back in a morphological way the various forms of consciousness developing in myth, philosophy, religion, mysticism, art and science to one single archetypal soul-spiritual form. This archetypal form, this 'proteus' of all human thought formation, he pictured as being in the self-experience of spirit through the experience of thinking, or respectively, in a human being's ego experience. (p. xxx)

According to Clement, Rudolf Steiner sees in the 'self-experience of the spirit'—in so far as it is a thought or ego experience—the archetypal form of 'all human thought formation'. But every thought *formation* presupposes the existence of a Being actively at work in *forming* thought. And who or what is this Being? Is it the 'spirit' that experiences 'self-awareness'? If this were so, what is spirit? There are a large number of possible conceptions of this. And what does Clement understand by 'experience of one's own self'?

According to Rudolf Steiner it is not enough that in 'going back' one goes only as far as the 'archetypal form [...] of all human thought formation.' He considers it essential to push on beyond every form to *that which forms it,* from every thought formation to *that which creates it.* What does the forming and the creating is *thinking.* All the concepts referred to by Clement—'spirit', 'thought formation', 'experiencing the self', etc.—all these presuppose thinking, which produces them. In order to know what the 'experience of thinking' is, I have to think about it, and this presupposes thinking. It is of the greatest importance that the point of departure for Rudolf Steiner's spiritual science is solely and alone *thinking* itself:

> I must lay special emphasis on the fact that people must notice at this point that I have *thinking* as my starting point, and not *concepts* and *ideas* that are gained through thinking. These presuppose that thinking is there first. Therefore what is said about thinking—its ability to exist in its own right, not be determined by anything else—cannot simply be transmitted to concepts. (*The Philosophy of Freedom* [1894], Chapter IV)

If you overlook the fact that the starting point of Rudolf Steiner's spiritual science is nothing but thinking, and not any of the concepts and ideas produced by thinking, then you will also overlook the fundamental fact that this kind of spiritual science can only be achieved by means of a *further development of thinking* towards a totally new kind of thinking activity.

The essential nature of the 'Steiner phenomenon' lies in the statement that human beings can develop their thinking. By means of such a further development, a source of knowledge of a different kind opens up—a source of knowledge that nobody had attained before Rudolf Steiner. Everything that is not perceivable by the senses, the whole content of 'myth, philosophy, religion', etc., can, according to Steiner, be experienced by thinking in *exactly the same way as we experience perceptions* of the objects of sense perception. Through a further development of thinking, we can come to see everything spiritual initially as a perception. With regard to this sort of perception, our thinking can be just as active as it is in relation to perception in the sense world.

In Clement's Introduction there is no mention of a further development of thinking to the point of perceiving in the spiritual realm. All the 'different forms of [...] consciousness' rank for him as different kinds of the type of 'thought formation' that is familiar to everyone. That is something essentially different from Steiner's statement, that perception in the spiritual realm is the beginning of spiritual knowledge. To speak about Steiner's spiritual science as though it had arisen through experiencing spirit in ourselves via normal consciousness, by means of the forming of thoughts known by everybody, means to misunderstand it totally. Without a substantial further development of thinking there is no objective knowledge of spiritual reality.

Steiner's *Philosophy of Freedom,* the basis of anthroposophy, deals with the *perception of thinking,* with 'thinking about thinking' as the means of perceiving it. Thinking is grasped as the only purely spiritual 'Being' (Rudolf Steiner) that is perceptible to ordinary consciousness. On the strength of such a percept and by creating the corresponding concept, there arises an objectively scientific knowledge of thinking as a purely spiritual reality. That is the beginning of a 'spiritual science' which, *by means of a further development of thinking,* knows besides the reality of thinking many other realities objectively, through perceiving them in the purely spiritual realm and by adding to these perceptions their concepts. The method here is the same as it is for natural science.

The 'spiritual researcher' does his research in the domain of spirit, just as the 'natural researcher' does his research in the realm of nature. The results of his research are no different or less assured than for the realm of natural science.

With Clement there is no mention at all of this entirely different kind of thinking. When he goes into the question of where the content of Steiner's book *Christianity as Mystical Fact* comes from, he sets out (on pp. xxx–xxxi) his own opinion about it, and relegates Steiner's statement on its origins to the modest position of a footnote. But let us give Steiner first place here:

> The spiritual knowledge that is acquired in *Christianity as Mystical Fact* has been drawn directly out of the spiritual world itself. Not until I came to show my audience during the course of a lecture, or my readers as they read my book, the harmony that existed between what I saw spiritually and the historical documents, did I draw on that and refer to it in my exposition. But I did not include anything in my account that was in those documents that I did not *beforehand* have in front on me in the spirit. (*Autobiography*, Chapter XXVI)

To this, Christian Clement says:

> On the one hand Steiner appears as a scholar, discussing documents that exist historically, factually interpreting authors, and on the other hand he claims, at least in biographical retrospect, above all to be speaking about his own mystical experience, and only to refer to other thinkers and theorems by way of illustration. (p. xxx)

Clement maintains that Steiner presents himself as a 'scholar'. This contradicts Steiner's statement that—entirely unlike a scholar—he is someone who describes what he has 'drawn directly out of the spiritual world itself', quite independently of any external source. There has never been a scholar previously who has claimed to be able to do this. Clement talks about Steiner 'discussing documents that exist historically, factually interpreting authors'. This again contradicts Steiner's avowed intention, to want to show 'the harmony that exists between what I saw spiritually and the historical documents'. All Steiner wants to do is simply 'insert' the documentary evidence where it belongs. According to him it is in no way his intention to 'discuss' them, and he has no intention of factually 'interpreting authors'. This is also due to the reason that he has no intention of inserting 'anything' from other authors 'that I did not *beforehand* have in front of me in the spirit'.

Clement goes on to say: '[. . .] he claims, at least in biographical retrospect, above all to be speaking about his own mystical experience'. To say 'above all' is a gross misrendering[3] of what Steiner writes. Steiner makes it clear that he didn't insert into his own writings 'anything' from other documents that he did not *beforehand* (Steiner's emphasis) see before him in the spirit. To call Steiner's inner experience simply a 'mystical experience' is highly misleading. If we refer to what Steiner 'claims', we have to be aware of the following. That, innumerable times—not just when he looked back in 'biographical retrospect'!—Steiner contrasted his inner experience, resulting from a further development of thinking, to every other sort of 'mystical experience' known previously. He presented these as opposite experiences. A mystical experience as such is characterized exactly by the fact that it has nothing to do with the sober element of thinking.

There is no doubt: Clement is purporting to portray in a factually objective way what Steiner 'claims for himself', but in reality he distorts Steiner's statements. The important thing about anthroposophy is its *scientific,* that is objective, knowledge of the spiritual world acquired by perception and thinking. In describing this method as the result of common 'human thought formation' or 'mystical experience' Clement sweeps Steiner's spiritual *science* from the table with a single stroke. The concept of spirit as a reality that can be known in an objectively scientific way, by means of perception and concept building, gets no mention in his Introduction.

On p. xxxii he summarizes anew his interpretation of the Steiner phenomenon. He speaks of 'Steiner's method of interpretation'. Here again he ignores the fact that Steiner's spiritual science is not the result of the interpretation of something or other, but exactly the opposite: original scientific research in the realm of spirit.

According to Clement, Steiner's method of interpretation should result from three factors (see p. xxxii). The first is the 'method of observing morphologically', in the sense of Goethe, and its 'application to the sphere of the soul and spirit'. It remains entirely open what happens when Goethe's theory of metamorphosis ceases to be a mere theory and becomes a real transformation of one's own soul and spirit. In the case of a plant, stem and leaf formation can be regarded as two metamorphoses of a growth that they both have in common. But to look at growth and decay, coming to life and withering, using the same concept of metamorphosis would be a distortion of the facts. Withering is not a metamorphosis of growth but only becomes possible when growth ceases to be. It is confusing to say that withering is a (further) metamorphosis of growing, death a metamorphosis of birth. It would be more suitable to describe these concepts as being like a turning inside out or a reversal. To describe ailing lungs as a metamorphosis of healthy ones does not tell us anything about why one form is 'healthy' and the other is exactly the opposite—'sick'.

Similar reflections apply to the second element that Clement sees in Steiner's method of interpretation, 'radical individualism'. This concept also remains just as abstract, totally indeterminate. In the sense of the 'ethical individualism' that Steiner talks about in his *Philosophy of Freedom*, it can either be properly understood or again misunderstood. The third element is presented in greater detail:

> Thirdly, Steiner's method of interpretation resulted from self-projection out of the mystical basic attitude itself: whoever regards the inner human being as the only place where the essence of all Being is revealed is, in the end, only being consistent if he tries to draw this Being out of his own ego, even when he undertakes to present the manifestation of this Being in the thinking of other personalities. So, in his works in 1901 and 1902 Steiner was consciously searching for [...] a subjectively and personally coloured [...] view of

> various forms of this Being in human consciousness. His aim [...] was to illustrate and legitimize the central postulate of the meaning of Self Knowledge as the place of origin of the ideas about the beyond and on nature in the evolution of culture. (p. xxxii)

These reflections, too, where no distinction between percept and concept is recognizable, are full of abstractions that only go to prove that the kind of thinking that, in the realm of the invisible lacks the unambiguous connection to the percept, can move in any direction whatever. Thus, in the first part of the quotation, Clement maintains that a 'self-projection' takes place, that one's own self projects itself actively into everything. This would exclude the possibility that 'Being is revealed' in an objective way, for whoever 'tries to draw "this Being out of his own ego" the contents that are "in the thinking of other personalities"' can only falsify them. In the second part of the quotation the exact opposite is maintained. What was previously something merely projected is now being presented as what is actively doing the projection, and vice versa. Clement had just been talking about the fact that one's own self transfers itself into everything by way of self-projection. Now, on the contrary, the Being of all things is described as projecting itself as an active agent into human consciousness and a contemplation of 'various forms of this Being in human consciousness' is taking place. This consciousness is now the opposite of an actively projecting one, consisting of nothing but projected images.

Once again it becomes clear that where there is no percept one can irrefutably maintain one thing or its opposite. All this is a confirmation for Clement that, where Steiner is concerned, everything remains 'consciously subjective and personal'. He maintains that Steiner takes pains 'consciously', knowingly, that where he is concerned nothing is objective or impersonal. Steiner, however, says exactly the opposite about himself, when for example he explains that in his spiritual science,

> The world is not presented as human ideas are within us. [...] The impressions are such that they are in fact experienced as being

> outside the human being. This is why these things are not understood by those people who can only experience ideas that lie within us, as is the case in the intellectual Age. [...] This Age perceives only what lives within the human being and projects it outwards. No one will ever in the most elementary way be able to describe an outer world [... as is done in my *spiritual science* ...], if one only projects outside what lives in man's inner being. (Compare GA[4] 207, p. 164. *Cosmosophy*, Vol. 1, lecture of 15 October 1921, Dornach)

In the course of many pages Clement does not tire of rubbing into his readers in numerous, at times long-winded repetitions of his interpretation of the Steiner phenomenon. For instance he says on p. xxxvi:

> This idea of an ultimate identity of 'world' and 'ego', of existence and consciousness, and the understanding of human freedom as the place of self-creation of the world being: those were the two 'root thoughts' gleaned from the German idealism [...] of Steiner's early philosophical works.

Here, too, the very thing of decisive importance to Steiner, and until today unique in humanity, is lacking: the experience and the concept of *a perception of what is spiritual*, that for our thinking possesses all the qualities of sense perception—above all the main quality of being, compared to thinking, something purely negative, an unreal image. So long as the 'identity of "world" and "ego"' is nowhere perceived—the opposite of what happens in Steiner's *Philosophy of Freedom* with respect to thinking—it remains a totally indeterminate and meaningless abstraction, allowing for every possible interpretation.

The percept is always concrete. Anyone whose thinking is based upon perceptions can only describe, depict or speak about what he, in each case, has perceived. The 'explanation' of something results no less from the many perceptions it presents, in its being and its acting, from every possible viewpoint. I do not actually ever perceive the 'world' or the 'ego', not even *the* birch leaf, but *this* particular birch leaf. And whenever I look at it, I perceive a different aspect of it: its colour, its form, one or another of its qualities—ad infinitum. Therefore, Steiner sees the further development of thinking primarily in becoming—and also in regard to spiritual realities—as realistic and many-sided as possible. But if thinking disregards perception, it can say what it likes, just because it cannot be checked by perception. Talking about 'world' and 'ego' and their final 'identity' says everything *and nothing*.

Through a further development of thinking there arises, according to Steiner, something opposite to thinking in the purely spiritual realm, similar to the situation in sense perception. This opposite, which Steiner calls Imagination, is like sense perception, the empty and unsubstantial picture of a reality. Thinking completes the spiritual perception with a concept, which Steiner calls an inspiration, just as it does in the case of a sensual one. At the same time, all the imaginative pictures that are being created must subsequently be made to disappear and a totally empty consciousness must be experienced before spirit can be grasped inspirationally. The awareness of a spiritual reality leads the perception in the supersensible (Imagination) and the forming of a concept by means of this perception (Inspiration) to an objective and intuitive recognition of Being (Intuition)—no differently than in the case of sense perception. All this prohibits describing perception and concept in the realm of spirit as being some kind of metamorphosis of the generally known forming of ideas that can only occur if based on sense perception.

Imagination, Inspiration and Intuition are for Steiner three different states of consciousness that can exist alongside the normal daytime consciousness, and that enable us to know three additional worlds that are unknown to ordinary consciousness. Even in his very last book, which was about medicine (the proofs of which he read only three days before his death), Steiner speaks about something 'perceived in a truly spiritual way'. He writes:

> It is a matter here of really looking at something—a spiritual perceiving—of something that has the reality of being. [...] To achieve

> this ability to perceive spiritually one cannot just continue to think indistinctively in the ordinary way as with the usual thinking; nor can one conjure up another world through the force of fantasy. On the contrary, we extend the human powers of cognition in an absolute exact way, and this extension leads to an experience of an expanded world. (GA 27, Chapter 1, p. 13. *Fundamentals of Therapy*)

Rudolf Steiner writes here with absolute clarity that the contents of his spiritual science are *not* acquired by means of forming ideas in a way that is possible for ordinary consciousness ('through the force of fantasy'). According to his report on his own spiritual experience, a human being at the stage of Imagination lives in a world that is different from the physical one—an 'etheric world', where the human 'etheric' or 'life body' is to be found. This etheric body is like a 'second human being' within the human being, whose perceptions cannot be memorised, because to do this one needs a physical organism. At the East-West Congress in Vienna in 1922 Rudolf Steiner explains the following about a spiritual researcher:

> He develops his observations about spiritual realities in such a way that he experiences them, but he cannot possibly make them into memories in the same way that he can make into memories the thoughts that are acquired from the outer world in our everyday life. [...] That is one of the most important features that guarantees the reality of a modern clairvoyance: that we don't unite with our bodily nature what we see spiritually. For them to be able to have a certain lasting value, our thoughts must unite with our bodily nature; they must be fortified through our physical organism. (Rudolf Steiner, *Leben in dritten Jahrtausend*, 2nd edn, 2014, pp. 94–5; text edition. GA 83, pp. 83–4, *The Tension Between East and West*)[5]

Correspondingly, the same applies to the 'astral' world and, for the 'third' human being in man, to the 'astral body' (the soul), as well as for the actual 'spiritual world', where the self (the I or the ego), that is the individual spirit of man, lives.

This is not the place for a more detailed discussion on the theory of cognition, which is found in archetypal form in the first part of Rudolf Steiner's *Philosophy of Freedom.* In this work the reader finds above all the overcoming of abstract intellectuality, which knows no difference between mental picture and percept. Steiner never tires of emphasizing that also in the case of a spiritual perception the object (the counterpart or opposite), which appears to be something outside, pretends to be or simulates a full reality which it neither has nor is. Intuitive thinking produces the concept, the side of reality which the percept lacks. It makes a full reality in dealing with the supersensible percept no differently from the way it does with sense perception. Seen this way, every mental picture—every formation of an idea—is nothing else but a percept that is seen looking at one's own inner being. Like every other perception it can only be made into full reality by means of thinking.

The inner path on which human beings develop thinking (and will) further, and arrive at objective knowledge of the spiritual world, has been described by Rudolf Steiner innumerable times in his books and lectures. His report on his own experience on the three levels of supersensible knowledge that we have mentioned, and the description of the inexhaustible contents he gained through them, gives evidence of a phenomenon in the development of human consciousness that today is still unique. Nowhere does Clement say a word about this unique fact, this epoch-making event. He describes the contents of Steiner's *Christianity* as though they had been acquired by means of the same avenues of knowledge that the thinker Hegel or the mystic Böhme had at their disposal. Those men, however, laid no claim to a 'spiritual science' that is of the same nature as natural science. Neither could they show an abundance of perceptions in the realm of spirit (imaginations), such as Steiner reported during his lifetime. Clement writes on p. lxxi:

> His [Steiner's] observations about antiquity and early Christianity, therefore, amount to pointing to himself and to his own work as to the goal of the spiritual evolution of the West. Just as Hegel a good hundred years before him, Steiner felt himself, at the latest around

> 1910, to be the bearer of Spirit developing in world evolution, which had found in him and his world-view its highest stage of development.

Clement sees in Steiner's spiritual science a world-view which, like all the others, arose purely speculatively, not as a view that arises from an essentially new way of thinking. To the very end, the central question remains untouched—the question of what Rudolf Steiner means when he says in his *Autobiography* that all the contents of his *Christianity* are 'taken directly from the spiritual world'? Clement only speaks of the kind of contact with the invisible world that everyone knows about. Nowhere in his reflections is there any mention of an objectively scientific knowledge of spiritual reality that is possible to reach solely by means of a further development of thinking, as Steiner claimed for himself. And because Clement doesn't know or accept such a new kind of knowledge he cannot bring to words his own implicit basic assumption—the assumption that the kind of thinking he knows is the only possible one.

There is also an understandable psychological reason for this. Such an assumption, once it has been made conscious and spoken out, would immediately show its impossibility and therefore its unscientific character. For it is impossible to prove scientifically that there cannot be a scientifically objective knowledge of the spiritual world by a further development of thinking—to prove that this cannot happen to anybody at any time. All one can say is that one does not know of such a manner of knowledge oneself, that one doesn't know from one's own experience what is meant by it—and that as a scientist one can only admit generally proven facts, and that one must otherwise keep silent.

Let us give a concrete example of something that Clement himself refers to. When Steiner speaks or writes about the childhood of Jesus, where did he get the content from? For Clement, there are only two possible sources: other authors and the kind of 'human thought forming' that are at everybody's disposal, or else 'mystic experience' as commonly understood. But Steiner excludes both these from bearing any weight when speaking of his own experiences. He says, rather, that his ability to check the contents of the four Gospels, and even add to them, is owed to his own direct research into the spiritual world by means of percept, concept forming and recognition of Beings. According to Steiner, everything that happened historically is available in its spiritual content. By perception and thinking it can be spiritually researched any time. To this, Clement says:

> At the same time he developed highly complex ideas about the composition of the bodily members of Jesus who bore the Christ: His 'astral body' was that of the Buddha who lived earlier, his 'etheric body' (at least part of it) was Adam's, and his 'ego' was Zarathustra's. And further, regarding the two family trees of Jesus outlined in the Gospels of Matthew and Luke [...] he postulated the existence of two Jesus children (and of two holy families) who, in a highly complicated process of mutual exchanges of their bodies, enabled the highly developed form of the Jesus boy [...] to be a suitable human bearer for the Christ. (p. lvi)

Clement's unspoken assumption applies here again that it is impossible for Steiner to come to know, by means of direct perception, either the spiritual nature of Christ or Jesus in an objectively scientific way. Steiner can only have 'developed' his highly complex 'ideas' with regards to the Christ spirit through the kind of idea forming that is available to everybody. He can only have 'postulated' the particular statements he makes; that is, he devised them intellectually or invented them.[6]

Steiner speaks of two Jesus children and of two corresponding families—the pious naming of the two families as 'holy' comes from Clement and not from Steiner. To put it succinctly, whether there have been one or two Jesus boys can only be decided upon by perception. The Gospel of Matthew speaks of a Jesus boy, and the Gospel of Luke also speaks of a Jesus boy. By looking more closely, by reading the two texts more attentively, we soon come to the conclusion that what the two texts say about Jesus has nothing in common. To take one example: in Matthew the Jesus boy flees to Egypt, where he lives for several years; the parents of the Luke Jesus boy return straight after his birth to Nazareth in Galilee, where he grows up. The important question for the academic, who is looking scientifically at the Bible from a historic point of view, is: can this be one and the same boy?

From his spiritual research, Rudolf Steiner points to the fact that both Matthew and Luke portray faithfully what they see in the realm of spirit. They see it by means of an inspired clairvoyance, in which the corresponding thoughts are given automatically with the pictures. Steiner can, out of his entirely new kind of spiritual research, only confirm in all their details what is written in both the Gospels. Clement totally misrepresents the phenomenon when he maintains that Steiner 'postulates' the existence of two Jesus boys by means of 'forging some Christological theory' (p. liv). According to Duden, a postulate is a 'thesis that has not been proved or is not provable'.[7]

Clement defines Steiner's 'ideas' about Jesus as 'highly complex' or 'highly complicated'. This is like blaming an anatomist for 'developing highly complex ideas about the composition' of the physical organism. Every reality that is looked at objectively, from as many aspects as possible, will show endless complexity, whether it is a sun system or a single rose. Something can only be 'highly complex' to someone who has difficulty in understanding. Clement argues like someone who is reprimanding an anatomist on two accounts: firstly, because he is 'postulating' a body, the existence of which cannot be proved; and secondly, because he is assuming this body to be 'highly complex', whereas in reality it is utterly simple.

This is all conceived with the same sort of logic with which Clement writes, in another place, 'impossible' to be a further intensification of 'improbable'. He even insinuates that Rudolf Steiner could have made Clement's 'idea'—according to which the physical reincarnation of Christ in Krishnamurti appears to be 'improbable', not to say 'impossible' (p. lvii)—his own. A sound human mind is clear about the fact that what is 'improbable' must be possible—it cannot be 'impossible'—and that what is 'impossible' can be neither probable nor 'improbable'.

In everything Clement affirms in his Introduction, there is only what a person—never mind whether he is called Clement, Steiner or anything else—thinks out in an intellectually rational way, i.e. abstractly speculating, without concerning himself about the side of *perception* in the matter. But if the element of perception is lacking, we are just as far away from reality as we would be if the concept was lacking—a core idea in Rudolf Steiner's *Philosophy of Freedom*. In purely intellectualistic abstraction, when the perception is disregarded, one can prove or refute anything, scot-free. Kant's antinomies of pure reason are a famous example of this.

When thinking gets out of the way of perception's unambiguous nature, it can claim to be right in every possible direction. This is the case when Clement writes that, in his *Philosophy of Freedom,* Steiner 'identified thinking as the element of the origin of the world'. (p. xliii) Each of the five concepts in this formulation can be interpreted in different directions, by making them more precise or by developing them according to one's needs. In this formulation, only statements about thinking can be checked via normal consciousness through the very perception of thinking. To check statements about the other four concepts one needs perception of the supersensible, which normal consciousness does not have.

This arbitrariness in giving proof also explains the fact that a series of eight volumes begins with Volume 5, where Clement asserts, among other things, that Steiner's *Mysticism* and *Christianity,* according to his own interpretation of *The Philosophy of Freedom,* are a follow-on from this work—although he doesn't give the reader any perception of his interpretation. Presumably, he is of the opinion that the reader has no need of it. That is to follow later, in Volume 2. And besides, when one begins a series of eight volumes with Volume 5, one can, later on in the 'preceding' Volumes 1 to 4, refute all the objections to Volume 5 by saying that—due to the lack of the preceding volumes—the reader has misunderstood the writer or failed to understand him at all.

Or let us take pp. xlvii–xlviii, where again Clement ignores that Steiner speaks unambiguously about his own perceptions in the spiritual realm, which are of *an entirely different nature* than all the other known kinds of idea-forming or mystical experience:

> And in his autobiography in 1924–25 he [Steiner] referred once again to this topic (topos), when he talked about his personal spiritual 'having stood before the Mystery of Golgotha in innermost and earnest cognitive celebration', and so joined the crowd of the direct witnesses of Christ's crucifixion, in the good old manner of Böhme.

Clement takes the word 'spiritual' out of the quotation from Steiner's *Autobiography*, although it belongs within it, and puts in his own word 'personal' before it, as though personal and spiritual mean the same thing. But it is not so: what is 'personal' is subjective, not in the least bit objective; and what is 'spiritual' is objective, not in the least bit subjective. What is personal is different in everybody; what is spiritual is the same for everybody. Every mental picture of a triangle is personal and subjective, different for everybody; the concept of the triangle is spiritual and objective—there is only *a single* concept of the triangle for everybody. If you equate 'personal' and 'spiritual', your thinking becomes so abstract that you can maintain anything you want to.

And as a result of this equating of 'personal' and 'spiritual'—of personally forming mental pictures subjectively, and objectively knowing spiritual truth—Rudolf Steiner, who forms his concepts and ideas about spiritual matters with the aid of *concrete spiritual perception*, is placed on a par with someone who, lacking spiritual perception, can only form *abstract and personal mental pictures* about spiritual realities—pictures that can only be formed with the aid of perceptions in the sense world.

Modern intellectuality overlooks the following all too easily: that *in thinking* human beings have a direct perception of a purely spiritual 'reality' (Rudolf Steiner), that is self-supporting and at the same time is an intuitively performed activity. It is only by way of the further development of thinking itself that any spiritual being can be grasped in its reality. The first step of this further development—the imaginative step—consists as mentioned previously in the *overcoming* of the illusion of the merely pictorial nature of the spiritual perception that, no differently from the sense perception, intrudes itself upon us as a full reality, without actually being it.

This explains why Clement calls the spiritual experience described by Steiner a 'topos'. A topos is like a fixed formula recurring in a number of people—'in good old bohemian manner'; 'the crowd of direct witnesses'—of a pattern of forming mental pictures. It is not the conceptual nature, the objective spiritual aspect of it that is important in a topos, but its pictorial or image character that belongs to what is 'personal' in the human being, not to what is 'spiritual'. Modern intellectualism, abstract rationalism, starts from the principle that there is only one kind of perception, which is sense perception. It sees everything else as a mental picture.

The unspoken dogma, that there cannot be an objective scientific knowledge of the reality of spirit, is the direct result of not understanding or ignoring altogether what spirit is. The only thing that intellectuality knows about spirit is its abstract and rationalistic mirroring within human consciousness, which Clement calls 'human thought forming', or 'mystical experience'. But such a mirroring is related to spiritual reality as a dead and void reflection is related to actively reflecting reality—as perception is to thinking.[8]

In Clement's Introduction to Volume 5, the specific nature of Rudolf Steiner's spiritual science is simply not recognized. Looked at psychologically one can see such a failed recognition as a repression, in the sense that it would be highly unpleasant to have to admit to oneself how ignorant an intellectual person is with regard to the reality of spirit, and how convenient it is not to have to tackle the further development of thinking that has become possible in modern times.

If one does not see that thinking, in order not to overstep its boundaries and lose itself in void abstraction, always needs the addition of perception, one will be tempted to disregard perception, also where sense perception is readily accessible. This is the case when Clement makes statements about Steiner's knowledge of Latin and Greek, without caring to see what Steiner himself says about this in his *Autobiography*. As a scientist, one can attempt, with the aid of facts, to refute or relativize what Steiner maintains, but no serious scientist should ignore it in writing about it. But since Clement does not acknowledge Steiner's original source of research, which is not dependent on any external source, he reproaches Steiner without further ado for not possessing the 'requisite scientific know-how for proper research' (p. xxxi).

Behaving as though he were a Steiner expert, Clement claims all sorts of things about Steiner, without giving visible evidence of what he says. It may be the custom in the academic world to begin a critical edition of a historically important work with a long introduction—but this has little to do with Clement's demand for 'proper source work, sharpness of method and a factual distance from the object' (p. xxxi). Altogether, Clement shows a lack of consciousness about his own limits in his venture as editor of works of spiritual science, of the uniqueness of the method and research that basically eludes him.

His presentation of Steiner's spiritual science is not only unscientific, but is also hostile to science. It would be scientific if Clement had articulated his implicit assumption—that the kind of knowledge he knows is the only possible one, that there cannot exist an objectively scientific knowledge of spiritual matters by means of a further development of thinking, as Steiner claims for himself—and on that basis tried to refute Steiner's claim about spiritual science as being built on an error or a self-deception. It is unscientific, however, not to make conscious one's own basic assumption, to give it implicitly the status of an irrefutable dogma and to misrepresent Steiner's spiritual science—to dismiss it by treating it as the result of the ordinary forming of mental pictures and theories. And it is furthermore hostile to science to set up one's own dogma as an authoritarian power that indicts being unscientific, and effectively ostracizes everyone who, like Steiner, does not fit in. In this way a person can try to hinder the arising of a scientific knowledge of the reality of spirit in present day humanity.

2

Are Faith and Spirit Merely a Private Concern?

An Attempt to Shelve Spiritual Science

In Christian Clement's appearance as editor of Rudolf Steiner's works, not only academic intellectualism plays a part but also religious conservatism, the kind that lives in the Mormon university where he is a professor.* The mention of funding by Brigham Young University (USA) of Volume 5 is placed prominently on the imprint page iv of the book. This is a significant symptom, pointing to the weight of the Mormon background behind Clement's work.†

BYU reportedly offers funding equally to all teaching fellows to help subsidize the publication of scientific and academic works. However, they are able to do this as the university chooses its personnel carefully. The Mormons sensibly only give

* In its lengthy entry on the university, Wikipedia states (December 2014) that Brigham Young is a private university, '... owned and operated by The Church of Jesus Christ of Latter-day Saints (LDS Church). [...] Approximately 98% of the university's 34,000 students are members of the LDS Church, and one-third of its American students come from within the state of Utah. BYU students are required to follow an honor code, which mandates behavior in line with LDS teachings such as academic honesty, adherence to dress and grooming standards, and abstinence from extramarital sex and from the consumption of drugs and alcohol. Many students (78% of men, 10% of women) take a two-year hiatus from their studies at some point to serve as Mormon missionaries. A BYU education is also less expensive than at similar private universities, since "a significant portion" of the cost of operating the university is subsidized by the church's tithing funds'. (Ed.)

† Christian Clement has stated: 'I am not a Mormon ... I am merely ['bloß'] a member of The Church of Jesus Christ of Latter-day Saints.' (Facebook, 17 October 2014)

their money to causes they want to promote. And where Rudolf Steiner is concerned they can, if they are honest and consistent with their belief, only want to promote one thing: the removal, or at least the shelving, of anthroposophy, as Clement tries to do in such an exemplary way in his Introduction. For anthroposophy considers all forms of old belief, in so far as they reject objective knowledge of the spirit, as being behind the times, as being a retarding factor, at a time when every human being is becoming capable of striving towards a scientific knowledge of the spirit by virtue of intuitively creative thinking.

This also underlines the significance of the biblical statement that is apparently inconspicuous, but in reality just as highly symptomatic as the one which Clement gives tone to in all his reflections. It takes up two whole pages (p. xxiii and p. xxiv) and is quoted in lapidary form—in the Greek original—so that enlightened people, who are for Clement and not so keen on Christianity, do not get to the gist of it too quickly. It is a statement from the Gospel of John: 'I and the Father are one' (p. xxiii):

> ἐγὼ καὶ ὁ πατὴρ ἕν ἐσμεν
> —John 10:30

In a multi-volume edition of historical-critical review that wants to be highly scientific, a simple Christian belief is being shown in a quite ostensible manner.

Some readers of the first edition of this book were surprised, as I spoke about this biblical statement from John's Gospel as though it were an expression of fundamentalist belief. These readers were of the opinion that Clement never appears as a believer, but writes in a purely scientific way. I do not question that this may also apply to his biblical quotation. Just look at this, he seems to say to anyone who is interested, even John's Gospel is of the opinion that the world (represented by the divine Father) is a self-projection of the ego, a product of human idea forming: I and the Father are one! On p. xxxvi of his Introduction he writes (as quoted on p. 14) of 'This idea of an ultimate identity of "world" and "ego" ...'

In these lines an emphasis has been laid on the fact that where there is no perception—as in the case of the relationship between the divine Father and the divine Son—abstract thinking can move absolutely freely in all directions. That for the *human* I the world is a self-projection can become true to an increasing extent through the further development of thinking, as more and more of the world contents become the intuitive content of human thinking itself. But precisely this perspective of the further development of thinking, by means of which this biblical quotation can become a truth, is never recognized by Clement as possible, let alone as being the specific essence of anthroposophy.

This biblical motto, which is quoted the American way, must be seen differently from the perspective of the elders or leaders of the Mormon Church, who are ultimately responsible for Brigham Young University.* If they are not frivolous or naive, they must consider Rudolf Steiner's anthroposophy, especially his Christology, as having the utmost significance. They must know that Steiner's spiritual science claims to reach objective truth in matters of spirit. What Clement writes about Steiner must be of the greatest importance to them.[9] It is quite impossible that it has eluded them that they have every reason to foster Clement's project, both spiritually and financially. For they can only see it as the greatest stroke of luck that academic science and Mormon faith are at one in proving that Steiner's Christology is just one form of 'theory building' among others, that it 'postulates' all kinds of things that have nothing to do with objective truth, with factual science.

Thus, at the beginning of Clement's Introduction, this striking picture has an immediate effect on the reader. Before Clement starts speaking as a scientist, through the biblical motto he is presented ostentatiously as a Christian believer. Firstly, a confessor of Christ, secondly, a dismantler of Rudolf Steiner! Seen

---

* The BYU website states that the university '... is wholly owned by the Church, which provides the University's principal source of funding from the tithing funds paid to the Church by its members. BYU draws its faculty and students principally from Church members.' (Ed.)

from the perspective of the Mormon faith, the message cannot be misheard or mistaken: science does not belong to spiritual matters. In matters of religion, faith alone has something to say. The basic conviction of an intellectual person, that there is no such thing as scientific knowledge of spiritual matters, is at the same time the dogma of a fundamentalist faith.

The attempt to shelve anthroposophy reveals itself as most undisguised where it concerns Christianity. Clement speaks of 'Steiner's Christological theory-building' (p. liv). He maintains that Steiner 'developed [...] highly complicated ideas' (p. liv) about Christ and Jesus; Steiner 'postulated [...] the existence of two Jesus boys' (p. lvi); Steiner 'presented himself as the direct source of immediate and unheard-of revelations' [...] (p. lvii).

The unqualified discourse on 'theory-building', of Steiner presenting himself as a source of 'unheard-of revelations', represents not only a misunderstanding of Rudolf Steiner and anthroposophy, but is at the same time a libel. All the talk about Steiner's 'theory-building', as explained in the first part of the book, has no objectively scientific basis. As for the 'revelations', all his life Steiner presented his spiritual science as the opposite of any kind of old-style revelation.

Human beings received revelations passively from the gods in olden times, when thoughts were given to them, alongside the words, through inspiration. In a totally opposite way, spiritual science arises through actively creative thinking. This presupposes the capacity for perceiving in the spirit realm by forming concepts through intuitive human thinking. Of course, the old revelation—as with Moses—was a direct experience of the spiritual world, but human beings could at that time not yet deal with it objectively and scientifically, that is freely, by way of perception and thinking. This is why these revelations had to come to an end. Human beings had to separate themselves in their consciousness from the spiritual realm, and perceive only sense percepts for a while—with the aim of receiving, with the aid of sense perception through natural science, a first training in thinking. Today we live at a time when human beings are striving, by means of a second stage of training, to go beyond the boundaries experienced at the initial stage of training. By means of perceiving in the spirit realm, we can build a spiritual science equal to natural science.

The two natural enemies of this spiritual science are modern intellectuality, with its claim that there cannot be any scientific knowledge of spiritual matters, and traditional religious belief, in so far as this rules out any claim to scientific knowledge of spiritual matters, labelling it to be people's wicked arrogance. In a Mormon university, academic intellectualism and religious conservatism work hand in hand. The same biblical quotation—'I and the Father are one'—can be understood and lived out simultaneously in two opposite directions: academically, intellectually, as testifying to the 'last identity of "world" and "ego"' (p. xxxvi); and piously, religiously, as a confession of the divinity of Christ as being of the same nature to God the Father (see p. xxiii). Rudolf Steiner's spiritual science should only keep its hands off Mormon belief!

Abstract intellectuality and religious faith both have in common modern materialism—the loss of the reality of spirit. To believe in spirit means not to experience it directly as spirit in thinking. An intellectual person has the full right to say to believers that all their ideas of the 'beyond', of 'God', 'Christ', etc., are merely human ideas, formed alongside sense perception and projected outwards. But the fact that the spirit of the believer is not real spirit does not mean that spirit does not exist. As long as human beings allow thinking to remain at the level it is now, there can be no reality of spirit for them. But Steiner's spiritual science exists within modern humanity as a proof that, by developing thinking further, one can intuitively become one with spirit beings.

It is a fact that more than a few of Steiner's followers see in his spiritual science another form of revelation to be believed in. But Clement does not act any differently when he reviles Steiner for presenting himself as a 'direct source of unheard-of revelations'. The only difference is that he rejects Steiner's revelations as tall stories whilst the others consider them genuine. With his talk of 'unheard-of revelations' he makes it clear that, for him, there are only two possibilities: to apply the only way of thinking he knows of, or to bluff. He all too clearly betrays the angry indignation of a scientist when Steiner evokes in him the slightest suspicion that he 'expresses himself all too vaguely, and by doing so, clothes himself in the aura of an "initiate"'. ('Commentary' p. 300)

By doing this, Clement portrays Steiner as being a kind of fibber—a great bluffer. Clement obviously has the right to do so, if that is his opinion. But the question arises here as to the *scientific quality* of a work that, according to Clement himself, is only given through an 'objective distance to the object' (p. xxxi). With regard to his postulated 'unheard-of revelations' of Steiner's, he shows an 'objective distance to the object' that is comparable to that of a bull to a red rag. No wonder that with his claim to 'sharpness of method' (p. xxxi) he can't grasp the uniqueness of Steiner's research method, and makes spiritual science out to be created by a kind of theory-building, which in reality is totally alien to it.

Such an attempt to obliterate anthroposophy doesn't have to be consciously intended. Clement himself takes his biblical motto from a Gospel that, as a matter of course, speaks of good and evil spirits that are at work in all human beings with different intensity. Spirits willing to destroy anthroposophy must know that their best instrument is human intellectuality—abstract rationalism—and that by taking no notice of perception they can 'prove' anything. Their will to exterminate spiritual science can be carried out best of all by human beings that people call brilliantly clever. In his *Mystery Dramas* Rudolf Steiner presented artistically the archetypal phenomenon of a brilliantly clever person—Ferdinand Reinecke. He is so extraordinarily clever that, with his power of reasoning, he is capable of shattering the confidence in thinking of a brilliant scientist like Strader.

Out of his spiritual research, Rudolf Steiner also points to the fact that all sorts of things can happen through a human being about which he himself hasn't a clue. Spiritual beings, who do have a clue, know all too well that the only chance of shattering anthroposophy in people's minds, including those of anthroposophists, is if the idea is instilled in sufficient numbers of people that they are doing everything they can to promote anthroposophy. To succeed in doing this, one must awaken in them the impression that they want to do all they can to foster the recognition of the merits of anthroposophy.

And it is not just a few people who hold the opinion that it is commendable service to anthroposophy that now, at long last, a critical edition of Rudolf Steiner's works is being edited by a professor from the USA, in line with the 'generally accepted standards of scientific work' (p. xxxi). Won't this be an honouring of Steiner's spiritual science, a glorifying of it? Won't anthroposophy finally be known more popularly once Steiner's works are introduced and commented on and stand on the shelves of university libraries? And, is it not highly welcome that someone undertakes to give the faultless and complete source references that Steiner omitted to give himself? Clement says to this:

> Faultless details about the sources, precision of method and unbiased distance to the object in the sense of the then and now generally recognized standards of scientific work were not Steiner's thing. (p. xxxi)

Such an assertion also arises out of ignoring Steiner's claim that he acquired the contents of his research directly from out of the spiritual world, quite independently from any outer source. And as to the scientific nature of his own work, Clements writes:

> A new standard edition is being set up here, from which all future anthroposophical research will have to take its bearings. (p. vxxvi)

In connection with the high 'standard' Clement claims for himself, one is permitted to ask the following questions. Is one allowed to use italics within the text that do not derive from the author? If words, sentences or whole paragraphs are printed in italics, should the reader not then think that they derive from the author and not from the editor? Shouldn't italics not deriving from the author himself be considered as misleading? Does the editor have no other technical know-how than to revert to imposing his own italics? This style in the chapter on Augustine in *Christianity* (pp. 223–8), just to mention one example, can perhaps be explained as being due to the missionary zeal of the editor, who uses italics to stress the great quantity of what Steiner has changed or added. But does it really show 'faultless details about the sources, precision of method and unbiased distance to the object'?

When Clement accuses Steiner of sloppy quoting of sources, he might consider the following. With the progress technology is making, there is an almost unlimited possibility to get hold of texts and to compare them. How would it be if a Professor X, with the help of his diligent assistants, undertook to prove that numerous formulations in Clement's texts are 'masked paraphrases' (p. xxxi), i.e. a plagiarism of other authors? Such a person could maintain that Clement 'paraphrased without naming his source' (as Clement does with Steiner, 'Commentary', p. 291). Clement could protest against this, but if there were a lot of people who believe Professor X rather than Professor Clement, it would look bad for Clement. We have a similar situation in regard to Clement and Steiner. Steiner maintains he has not taken anything from other authors, but Clement claims to have proved that he has, and that now and then he has even done so 'without naming his source'. It is clear to see that there are enough people, also among anthroposophists, who believe Christian Clement rather than Rudolf Steiner.

When I pick up Volume 5 of the SKA, I have before me the following picture. I see myself once again as a young man in New York many years ago, where I often led the 'farewell to the dead' in funeral homes. The person who had just died was laid out in such a way as to give the impression of being still alive. His make-up was so perfect, so 'ennobled' (see p. 46), that he appeared to be more alive than in life. His cheeks were rosier than I had ever seen them when he was still alive.

I see in this Volume 5, edited by the new editor of Rudolf Steiner's works, Christian Clement, the ritual of an academic burial of anthroposophy. The two side walls of this wonderful coffin are the 'Introduction' and the 'Commentary'—to which the dark grey colour of the case is well matched. The coffin nails of the Introduction are supplied by the repeated hammering of the protestation that there is nothing—nothing—and again nothing at all in the spiritual science of Rudolf Steiner. And the hammer blows of his 'Commentary' reinforce it bit by bit: there is not even a scientific discipline with the sources. The header and footer of the coffin are excellently fitted out on the one side by the imprint of the Mormon University's money and the cooperation of the Rudolf Steiner Verlag,* and on the other side by the believer's quotation from the Gospel that gives the Introduction its spiritual tone.

The corpse laid to rest in the coffin is Rudolf Steiner's anthroposophy, represented by two of his works. These are so perfectly edited in a historical-critical way that one can get the impression that Steiner is still alive. But the meticulously critical apparatus makes it clear that Steiner is long dead, to the point that he has become history. A deceased person can be forgiven for sending out 'unheard-of revelations' that are beyond good and evil, so long as one takes seriously the duty of an academic scientist to deal with them with 'unbiased distance to the object', that is, with a critical distancing under a magnifying glass.

And thus it is. Even if one were to manage to ignore the Introduction, the Commentary, the Mormon funding and the biblical quotation in order to concentrate on Steiner's texts with their thousands upon thousands of details fed into the critical apparatus, not only relevant to the texts but also concerning orthography and punctuation—to which also belongs the utterly

* Volume 5 of the *Kritische Ausgabe* ('Critical Edition') has been published by the German academic house Frommann-Holzboog, who initiated the project. However, it has been 'co-published' (in cooperation) with Rudolf Steiner Verlag, Basel, Switzerland. This co-publishing deal was discontinued after the first volume, evidently due to negative public reaction. (Ed.)

important matter of whether there is a full stop or not at the end of a title—after all this one has absolutely no time or energy left, should one still want to give Steiner's thoughts a chance to come to life in one's own mind and in one's own heart. In fact, the claim that one can find any real life in an academic context is ridiculous. The point of scientific research on a text is that a critical judgement has to be made—with an emphasis on 'critical'—if the work is to have any claim of being scientific. And you can only apply criticism if you prove your superiority to the text you are criticizing.

The reader should not misunderstand me. By speaking of an attempt to put anthroposophy into a coffin, I do not mean that there is any real possibility of shelving it. Anthroposophy is something spiritual, and so everything applies to it that also applies to spiritual reality: it is not perceptible to the senses, so it cannot die. Two thousand years ago, those who sought the spirit at the grave of the corpse of its bearer, at the place of the burial, were given the spiritual message: Him whom you seek is not here. He lives immortally as spirit.

* * *

To understand Clement's Introduction better, it can be helpful, if only by having a spotlight or two thrown on it, to follow the development of his way of thinking leading up to this point. His basic, unspoken assumption, that there cannot be such a thing as a scientific knowledge of spiritual realities, doesn't appear for the first time in his Introduction.

An important source for following Clement's process of thought is his aforementioned dissertation *Die Geburt des modernen Mysteriendramas aus dem Geiste Weimars* ('The Birth of the Modern Mystery Drama from out of the Spirit of Weimar'), Logos Press, Berlin 2007. In the framework of this book I have only been able to sketch with a few strokes the function of the 'percept' in spiritual matters ('Imagination'). On pp. 49–50 of his book there are important references to Imagination that allow us to look more deeply into Clement's way of thinking. He explains:

> In order to show the continuity in Steiner's thinking, one can try to interpret the anthroposophical theory of Imaginations by way of his philosophical works. *The Philosophy of Freedom* described knowledge as a process of the mutual interpenetration of percept and concept [...].
>
> So we can describe the Imagination in the terminology of *The Philosophy of Freedom* by calling it the condensing into pictures of the inner view of those soul/spiritual processes that in ordinary consciousness become deadened into the ideas of an outer world of the senses.

Clement speaks of 'the mutual interpenetration' of percept and concept. That is misleading, in so far as neither the percept nor the concept does the active penetrating, but solely thinking itself. Perceiving is, for the human being, like momentarily falling out of thinking, like a gentle dreaming or falling asleep. Thinking is like an awakening through active concept forming—an awakening to the reality of spirit that is beyond space and time.

In the second part of the quotation that has been presented, it becomes clear that Clement considers 'Imagination' not as a percept in the spiritual realm, but equates it with the whole process of knowledge.[10] But according to Steiner, Imagination is not an 'inner seeing' where the soul/spiritual processes 'have been condensed into pictures', but the very opposite. No less than sense perception, the imagination must be recognized in its fundamental character as a deception. Thinking should recognize in Imagination something like a dreaming, like a falling away from reality, and see its task to be, even with regard to Imagination, to create spiritual reality. Therefore Steiner stresses time and again that everything that has first been imagined has to be 'got rid of', and a 'totally empty consciousness' must be established in its stead. Between Imagination and Inspiration there is no continuity. No further metamorphosis of the imagination takes place, but a qualitative jump—a turning inside out or a reversal (see p. 12).

Here it becomes clear once more that all that abstract intellectuality can know about the supersensible realm is what it can think about it. But this, compared to thinking itself, is a pure world of percept, and can only become a full reality due to thinking. To put it more simply, on p. 22 of his dissertation Clement quotes Steiner as saying: 'If we want to envisage evolution as it is beheld in the spiritual world [...]'. The word 'beheld' points clearly to a perceiving in the spiritual realm, which in Steiner's case is no mere visionary seeing, or something that remains mere Imagination, but is a kind of perceiving imbued with thinking in the supersensible realm. Clement comments (p. 23):

> So Steiner is not looking for 'the human element we all have in common', the 'human being as such', he is not looking for 'spirit' in an abstract Absolute *beyond* individual personal experience, as Hegel did, but precisely *within* it.

Steiner's unambiguous reference to perceiving in the spiritual realm is not recognized, or else ignored, through Clement's turn of phrase, i.e.: 'Steiner is not looking for'.

Summarizing his discussions on the first scene of the first Mystery Drama, Clement writes in the original version of his doctorate (p. 227):

> [...] with this in *The Portal of Initiation* a twelve-fold archetype of man is being postulated. This is how Steiner realizes his conception of Drama as a presentation of the human element that we all have in common: This conception of the drama [...].

Clement maintains here, too, that Steiner perceived nothing directly in the spiritual domain. He was only equipped with the capacity, which is at every human being's disposal, to 'postulate' things or to devise a 'conception'. What holds true here, too, is that Clement's treatment of anthroposophy is missing any real scientific investigation by dogmatically excluding what is specific to Steiner's source of knowledge.

A few years later, in an essay called '"An open secret" or "secret revelation"? Goethe's Fairy Tale and the Apocalypse' (in: *Goethe's Yearbook*, Volume 17, 2010, published by North American Goethe Society, p. 254, Footnote 11), Clement points to Steiner's 'common features' to his own reflections on Goethe's *Fairy Tale*. He writes that Steiner had undertaken 'detailed analyses' which, even if they are 'inestimable', are only 'honoured as a preliminary work to the interpretation of the fairy tale presented here [by Clement]'. The talk of 'preliminary' work only makes sense if Clement sees Steiner as being on the same level as himself, if at all.

In the book *Weimar Classicism*, edited by David Gallagher (The Edwin Mellen Press, 2010), Christian Clement writes about Steiner's Mystery Dramas (in Chapter 6, 'Weimar Classicism Reincarnated: Rudolf Steiner's Theatre of Spiritual Realism'). In this book a number of academic scientists write articles about authors such as Goethe, Schiller, Forster and Berlepsch. What strikes us here regarding Steiner is that he appears to be quite unimportant. If we look more closely at what Clement writes about Steiner, we see the reason for this lack of importance: Steiner is presented as a dramatist who distinguishes himself only through his inferior quality.

Clement calls the Mystery Dramas 'abstruse' (p. 135). After defining Steiner as 'an Austrian philosopher and spiritualist', he writes:

> Another outgrowth[11] of his years defending and writing about Goethe is a series of four abstruse[12] mystery plays known as the *Mysteriendramen* (1910–1913). (p. 135)[*]

If we see Steiner's Mystery Dramas solely as the product of what Clement in his Introduction to Volume 5 of *SKA* calls 'human idea-forming', we could perhaps call them 'abstruse' in English. But, if we take our departure from the fact that their contents are obtained objectively, scientifically and with the aid of perceiving the spiritual, we will find everything in the Mystery Dramas to be presented simply and unaffectedly. From each person's endlessly complex life only a few experi-

[*] This text appears in the original English. (Ed.)

ences are chosen, and these are presented in a few characteristic strokes. For instance, the character Ferdinand Reinecke, whom we mentioned earlier, was not invented through 'abstruse' idea-forming, but, as Steiner himself says, was perceived spiritually as an objective reality. Why is he actually the one who wins against the character Strader? Because Strader, through his marriage to Theodora, lives a life where knowledge and belief, science and religion, live side by side but never become a unity.

As Clement gives credit only to idea-forming, which every dramatist has at his disposal, it is apparent as to why he can see none of Steiner's objectively perceived spiritual realities in the four kings in Goethe's *Fairy Tale*. They 'represent' for Clement merely 'symbolically', 'mental' human qualities.

> From their dialogues it is obvious that they are representations of human mental faculties: the gold king represents intellectuality and thought, the silver king symbolizes emotionality and feeling, while the former bronze king stands for intentionality and will. (*Weimar Classicism*, p. 140)*

Even in his discussion of the lectures on 'Speech Formation and Dramatic Art', which Steiner held at the end of his life (September 1924), Clement is a long way from conceding that Steiner lays claim to an objectively scientific knowledge of the spiritual world. We see clearly how Clement misunderstands the reality of spirit in the example of the vowels and the consonants. According to Steiner, the vowels are an expression of inner soul experiences and the consonants an expression of objective spiritual reality. Clement turns Steiner's thoughts into their exact opposite, when he maintains that the consonants are no less an expression of soul experiences.

> While Steiner sees the vowels as an expression of certain '*innerseelischem Erleben*' [soul experience], consonants are interpreted as '*geistige Gebärden*' [mental gestures] which serve the function of

*This text appears in the original English.

> structuring those soul experiences in time and space. (*Weimar Classicism*, p. 149)*

Clement's statement that Steiner intellectually or rationally 'interprets' what the consonants are meant to signify is wrong. By making such a statement he once again misses the fact that what is essential and new about Steiner lies in his further development of thinking to the stage of objectively and scientifically knowing the reality of spirit, arrived at through perception and thinking.

All in all, Rudolf Steiner is measured by the extent to which he remains true to Weimer Classicism. Despite all 'deviations from and misinterpretations of Goethe and Schiller', which Clement does not name, he acknowledges that Steiner has 'remained true to the intellectual and spiritual core of Weimar Classicism'.

> [...] Steiner's theatre of *Spiritual Realism* seems indeed, despite all his actual deviations from and misinterpretations of Goethe and Schiller which we did not mention here, to be true to the intellectual and spiritual core of Weimar Classicism.†

In another assessment of Steiner's ability as a playwright, he writes:

> Despite a huge ballast of esoteric theorems and an unarguable lack of dramatic and artistic maturity [...] But Steiner was, of course, no experienced playwright like Schikaneder [...]. (*Weimar Classicism*, p. 153)‡

This sort of thing can only be written frankly and honestly by someone who attributes to himself both artistic maturity and experience—and who knows what they are!

The express statements (points 1 and 2, below) and the implicit assumption (3) made by Clement in regard to Steiner's Mystery Dramas can be summarized as follows:

---

* Ibid.

† Ibid.

‡ Ibid.

1. Steiner's Mystery Dramas are an 'abstruse' product of the idea forming of a simple dramatist.
2. Steiner is 'indisputably'—i.e. it neither can nor may be disputed—an inexperienced and immature playwright, who in addition frequently misinterprets both Goethe and Schiller.
3. Steiner's assertion that he obtains the contents of his Mystery Dramas by perception directly out of the spiritual world is based on an error, a deception even.

Just as I, with all seriousness, see the academic entombment of anthroposophy being performed via Volume 5 of Clement's *SKA* (which features two of Rudolf Steiner's works), I see in his chapter in his book *Weimar Classicism* the perfect academic burial of Rudolf Steiner himself. He is being finished off, with all his insignificance and mediocrity, as a *quantité négligeable,* by a professor of a Mormon university who ranks as a 'Steiner expert'. This is saying nothing of Christian Clement's personal intentions, but is an observation of how, according to my personal conviction and experience, such a literary contribution works in the academic world and beyond.

There is no question about it: the representatives of the academic world and of traditional religion have every reason to celebrate Christian Clement and to promote him in every possible way. They can only rejoice if anthroposophy is dismissed as an abstruse form of theory-building and as an unheard of revelation by an immature artist. Western culture demands a strict separation between knowledge and belief. Knowledge only applies to the physical world, and science controls public life. Faith alone applies to the spiritual world, which should only play a part in private life. The regaining of the reality of spirit through spiritual science is, for both scientist and believer, the strongest challenge, especially since it abolishes the division between science and faith.

Many a reader will perhaps ask themselves why such weight is being given here to Christian Clement's 'critical edition' of Rudolf Steiner's work. There are two principal reasons for this.

Firstly, Clement's work is representative of the materialistically based intellectuality of science, which Rudolf Steiner—as we shall see in the next chapter of this book—perceives to be the main cause of the moral and social decline of humanity today. Intellectualism is the father of materialism, because it credits us with having scientific knowledge only of the physical world. Where the spiritual is concerned, it acknowledges only faith, which is permitted to play a role solely in private life.

Secondly, quite a few official representatives of anthroposophy renounce the defence of spiritual science in public, through word and deed. These individuals welcome and praise Clement's achievement as though it were fostering spiritual science. This makes anthroposophy's task harder than ever, as Steiner's words below clearly show.

> It could possibly happen that at some time anthroposophy would have to separate from the Anthroposophical Society. This ought not to happen, but the possibility will be there. Sometime in the future, when I am no longer here, an intellectualizing of anthroposophy will occur. Therein lies a great danger, for this would mean the stagnation of the whole movement.*

* From the book *Erinnerungen an Rudolf Steiner* (Verlag Freies Geistesleben 1979, p. 237), the article by Adelheid Petersen entitled 'Rudolf Steiner über Vortragstätigkeit und Zweigarbeit'. Petersen says of the quotation: 'There are two other assertions which Rudolf Steiner made elsewhere and repeatedly at that time [1919], one of which runs as follows.'

3

Does Anthropsophy Have a Future?

Intellectuality and Human Beings in Search of Spirit

Volume 5 of the *Schriften – Kritische Ausgabe (SKA)*, which we have discussed above, was published in August 2013 by Frommann-Holzboog Verlag in cooperation with Rudolf Steiner Verlag. In co-publishing the project, the Rudolf Steiner Verlag and Nachlassverwaltung (estate) become co-responsible for this 'critical edition' of the works of Rudolf Steiner, with its editor Christian Clement. In effect, then, this edition is an 'official' publication representing Rudolf Steiner's estate.* Referring to this at the beginning of 2013, the current director of the Rudolf Steiner estate, David Marc Hoffmann, wrote in categorical terms:

> Clement will be able to inspect texts here, but not be allowed to publish them, for, understandably, we want to keep them for a critical edition of our own. In so far as we do this, he will not be able to publish a historically critical edition himself, either. [...] On the other hand I have the impression that his edition will be a prolegomenon, a kind of forerunner to a critical edition that *we ourselves* will do in the future. (*Der Europäer*, February 2013, p. 30)

Just a few months later, however, and apparently in connection with his reading of Clement's Introduction to Volume 5 of *SKA* it was reported in *The Goetheanum* (13 July 2013, 'Die Schriften in ihrer Entwicklung' – 'The documents and how they came about') that the director of the Rudolf Steiner Archive, who acts on

*For readers who are unaware, Rudolf Steiner left his literary works and copyright to his wife Marie Steiner, who in turn set up the Rudolf Steiner Nachlassverwaltung to edit and publish Rudolf Steiner's works in the original German. Thus, Rudolf Steiner deliberately left his literary works to an individual and not to the Anthroposophical Society. (Ed.)

behalf of the Rudolf Steiner Estate, had 'recommended [Clement's] project to the Rudolf Steiner Verlag'. Hoffmann described *SKA* as 'ennobling' the works of Rudolf Steiner (see p. 34), and added that 'supplementary volumes' could be added to the 'critical edition' at a later date by the Rudolf Steiner Estate.

A few months earlier it had been stated that Clement could only publish a modest 'forerunner' to the announced forthcoming critical edition by the Rudolf Steiner Estate. Now, the Rudolf Steiner Estate was planning to add some modest 'supplementary volumes' to Clement's own edition, which they appeared to be celebrating. And what are the reasons for this strategic turnaround, with its unforeseeable consequences? Presumably, the Rudolf Steiner Estate had had second thoughts, more realistic ones, as to whether it was in a position to create its own critical edition of Steiner's *Mysticism at the Dawn of the Modern Age* and *Christianity as Mystical Fact* volumes (GA 7 and GA 8) that would be an improvement on Christian Clement's. Although it would have been their job to create such volumes, they hadn't done so in the hundred or so years since their initial publications.

But there is another, more important reason. There exists in the anthroposophical world an ever increasing movement that sees it as critical for the thriving of anthroposophy that it should be recognized, not only by the civil population but, above all, by the academic world. But in this hope lies the greatest dilemma for everybody who in our time is seriously interested in anthroposophy.

In order to integrate Rudolf Steiner's anthroposophy into its scientific tradition, the academic world would quite literally have to renounce its claim to absolute cultural dominance. Academia, and contemporary science, research phenomena by looking for causal explanations in the sense-perceptible world. For the spiritual scientist there appear in this world only the effects of causes, all of which lie in a world that is not sense perceptible. But lacking this perception, academic intellectuality can only speculate abstractly on matters of spirit, finding no objective reality in it.

So the question arises: what can modern medicine say to Steiner's statement that the heart is not a pump, i.e. that blood is not set in motion by the heart, but directly by a human being's spirit?

> [...] the heart exerts no activity with regard to the movement of the blood. Present-day natural scientists become livid when one speaks of such a thing. Years ago I once [...] explained this to a naturalist, a physician, and he became almost raving mad about the fact that we ought not to think of the heart as a pump any more, but that it is the blood itself that is propelled into movement by its own vitality [...]. (GA 205, pp. 104–5. *Therapeutic Insights*, lecture of 2 July 1921, Dornach, Mercury Press, 1984)

And what can the academic world say when Steiner, speaking in Torquay, states that, whilst investigating the behaviour of a sleep walker or a medium, a psychologist ends up talking nonsense about the phenomenon as he or she doesn't know what is happening with the person's spirit to cause their outer behaviour? Or when Steiner asserts that in order to really understand Woodrow Wilson, President of the USA, one should look back to his earlier life as Muawiyah in the seventh century? Shortly after Wilson's death, on 12 April 1924, Steiner said:

> [...] how can it make sense to discuss with anyone from today's contemporary civilization that the soul of Muawiyah has reappeared in the soul of Woodrow Wilson? [...] By way of argument, one would get nowhere. [...] One should not allow oneself to have the illusion that one can discuss such things. They should become known through their own strength and power. Such things are not to be resolved by dialectics. (See GA 236, p. 32. *Karmic Relationships*, Vol. II)

The only sensible thing the academic world can do in relation to Rudolf Steiner is to ignore him. This is what it has consistently done up to now.[13] In a lecture given on 23 May 1922, which did not find its way into print until 81 years later, Rudolf Steiner states that anyone who thinks academia would be able to accept anthroposophy is out of touch with the world:

> This way of being out of touch with the world is what has harmed us so very much in recent years, and we just have to overcome it. We should never fancy that we can spread anthroposophy with the aid of academics and scholars. We ought to be clear about the fact that specialized expertise will never accept anthroposophy on its own, but will have to be forced by outer circumstances. (See GA 255b, p. 356)

Such words make it clear that, according to Steiner, it is impossible for the academic world to accept anthroposophy. It is beyond the realm of competence of the academic sector. Clement's presentation of anthroposophy, however, is *not* impossible for the academic world, because he ignores its special feature, its claim to having scientific knowledge of the objective truth about the spiritual world.

There is another important matter here, too, that we ought to consider. Whilst academic science has limited itself to investigating the physical world, its research has become more and more exact and complex. This has brought about an increased emphasis on an outer, formal perfection which remains external and estranged to the subject matter. Clement's *SKA* is a typical example of this. Whilst going through the text, the fluctuations in orthography and punctuation are given the same weight as the differences relating to content.

Anyone wanting to bring a text to life would be grateful for even the smallest reference to its development, relating to meaning and content. But it is quite different when it comes to technical questions such as spelling and punctuation, which can be felt as an unbearable disruption, as a devious distraction. In fact, if one sees the text as spiritual nourishment, such commentary would inevitably be so. But Professor Clement has to deliberate on orthografy—pardon, orthography!—in a formally perfect way, in order to comply with the academic standards. He is quite right when he says that the world of academic science demands absolute exactness in recording even the most trivial of textual differences. He is right when he maintains that Steiner lacks such exactitude. The fact that Steiner even mentions 'sources' that should not be sources for him is simply nonsense to the present-day tribunal of academic science.

We can understand why, during his whole lifetime, Rudolf Steiner had trouble with representatives of both science and religion, and why they were often hostile to him. But what is unique about Christian Clement is that he is not only an exponent of the academic world, but also a representative of a religiously based academic institution. If he, we may ask, as an academic scientist were to present Steiner's anthroposophy as the necessary supplement to natural science with the same claim of scientific exactitude, wouldn't he make his position in the academic world, to which he belongs, untenable? And if he were to present anthroposophy, including what concerns Christianity, as a spiritual science with a claim to objectivity, instead of scorning it as a source of 'unheard-of revelations', would he ever have been appointed as a professor at a Mormon university?

Abstract intellectuality looks at the theoretical content of Rudolf Steiner's texts and thinks that to be the most important part. It is not concerned about the aspect that is much more important than the content, which is the effect that such content has on humanity. Does it have some effect, or is it as good as dead? Does it become an inner force in people? Does it help in shaping life? Or are the library shelves on which these books stand their cemetery—shelves full of 'tins of preserves', as Steiner calls them? A cookery book only makes sense if it leads to the living activity of cooking. Rudolf Steiner's anthroposophy only makes sense if it comes directly to life.

But the academic world must put the greatest stress on formal perfection. In a historically critical edition, everything has to be absolutely exact, which means, in effect, dead! What is alive can never be 'exact', cannot be perfectly scientifically objectified. That is only possible with things that are dead. In its striving for formal perfection, intellectuality itself is the other side of the 'estrangement from the world' that Rudolf Steiner speaks about. It sees as important only the theoretical content of a text, and does not take seriously the various contexts in real life in which it is placed. It does not see that a work by Rudolf Steiner can be dead in one life context and become alive in another. Whether it is shelved or brought to life in the milieu in which it finds itself is far more important than the theoretical content!

Rudolf Steiner explains this quite openly in a public lecture given on 30 October 1919 in Zurich:

> What holds us back is usually only cowardice, our lack of courage. [...] In outer life we are convinced, today, that we are practical, but we do not look at things so as to recognize them in their real nature. If we are presented with some statement, we deal with it by looking only at the abstract content of it. This can estrange us from life. [...] The point, today, is not that we agree with something's literal content, but that we acquire a judgement about the way the content is connected with reality. [...] Because people do not feel the need always to push on beyond the literal content to the actual reality is why they so often fail to judge it correctly. They don't try to go into the matter at all. People are satisfied with what serves as a top layer to life and covers up the true reality. To go all out to find true reality is the first and foremost requirement of our time. [...] If we take this throne speech [of Emperor Karl, 1917] from the beginning to the end, looking merely at the literal words superficially, it is a wonderful achievement with a *feuilletoniste* style. [...] But just look at the reality. Try to put the nice theory into its life setting. You have to ask: Who is saying this? What sort of place does he say it in? [...] What does the literal talk about democracy mean, however nice it is, in such a context? It is a great historic lie! Today we have to go back from the literal content of something to looking at the reality. We must not only grasp the contents with our intellect, we have to delve into reality. This is what spiritual science demands. (Rudolf Steiner, *Eine Menschheit* (2nd edn, 2012, pp. 34–7; or GA 332a, pp. 203–6. *The Social Future,* Lecture of 30 October 1919, Zurich)

Christian Clement's life context also has an influence on the way his Steiner 'critical edition' works in the world. As already mentioned, not only does academic science, which can only ignore anthroposophy, work through him, but also he is surrounded by religious fundamentalist ideas, and this can have no other intention but to get rid of anthroposophy, to put it aside. When Clement quotes the Gospel of John, the theoretical content of the quotation is of less importance than its connection with the Mormon milieu within which Professor Clement works. One should not forget that the Mormon sect is so powerful that it supplied the Republican candidate (Mitt Romney) in the last presidential election in the USA.

Professor Clement's success can be explained through the fact that in western culture public life is governed by the intellectuality of science, by the rationalism of progress, by science and technology. The conservative belief of religion applies only to private life. That intellectuality has also entered deeply into the world of anthroposophy is seen in the fact that, with Volume 5 of his *SKA*, Clement has secured for himself the favour of both the Rudolf Steiner Estate and of the Anthroposophical Society.[14]

The Anthroposophical Society in Germany, too, gives Christian Clement high praise, via editor Andreas Neider in *Mitteilungen aus der anthroposophischen Arbeit in Deutschland* (10/2013, p. 7):

> The most important thing for Clement, and this is made especially clear in his outstandingly formulated Introduction with its overview of the whole work. [...] And so he comes in his Introduction to his very well-founded conclusion that not only Steiner's way of looking at things comes from perceptive thinking [...] but that even Steiner's own path of development is founded on a life impulse that is based on the concept of metamorphosis.

Such a characterization says nothing about Steiner's special qualities—that he is the first, and up to now the only, spiritual scientist humanity has ever had—in whom 'perceptive thinking' has become perception in the spiritual realm, and the 'idea of metamorphosis' has become a unique metamorphosis of thinking itself.

The leadership of the Rudolf Steiner Estate appears to share this spirit of Christian Clement. For example, it points to Steiner's inner development and that he, supposedly, frequently changed his mind. In its editorial input to *Geisteswissenshaftliche Menschenkunde* (GA 107, 2011, pp. 340–1) they state in relation to reproaches against Steiner of racism that '... the publisher distances himself from such statements ...' However, it is unclear from what, exactly, the Estate is distancing itself from, because it also protests that Rudolf Steiner is not a racist. The editor maintains further that in 1909—the year when Rudolf Steiner, as he stated in Torquay on 20 August 1924, finished writing his *Occult Science, An Outline*—Steiner was still formulating 'sketches' on the race problem that had a 'provisional character' and contained 'points of view' that later on he considerably 'altered'. If that were true, then Rudolf Steiner's anthroposophy—much in accord with Clement's version—would be a world-view like every other, which in the course of its development passes through all kinds of changes and corrections, and can lay no claim to being objectively true.

As a further example, the current director of the Rudolf Steiner Estate, writing in the *Archivemagazine* (December 2013, p. 166), quotes from Rudolf Steiner's *Autobiography* (Chapter XXXV):

> Anyone who wants to pursue my own inner struggle and work in presenting anthroposophy to the consciousness of the present time must do so by the means of my written works.

Rudolf Steiner talks about his struggle 'in presenting', meaning the form of presentation of anthroposophy, as is made clear through the lengthy quotation we have given in our Preface. However, Rudolf Steiner's statement about his struggle is now made into *two struggles*:

> His own inner struggle and simultaneously the confrontation with the struggle for knowledge of his time [...].

His 'own inner struggle', apparently, should be seen in the alleged continual changing of Steiner's mind and the supposed evolution of his thinking; and besides this struggle—'simultaneously with it'—a second struggle was apparently going on, 'the confrontation' with the outer world.

The dilemma referred to, in which every human being with an enquiring mind finds himself today, has, in the course of time, brought about among anthroposophists two separate camps that are becoming more and more opposed to one another. One of them is doing all it can to make anthroposophy acceptable to both the general public and the academic world. But in order to do this it has to compete with the pervading intellectuality and to fight with the same weapons of abstraction. It can only succeed in this, as Clement's Introduction conclusively proves, when less and less of the content of anthroposophy remains. The others shy away from this insufferable watering down. They consider humanity either immature or unwilling to take up anthroposophy; therefore, they cultivate it as a purely private matter, away from all publicity.

That the stream of those open to the world have, in the course of time, become more and more powerful, is evident for one thing in the victory of this one tendency within the Executive Council (*Vorstand*) of the Anthroposophical Society in Dornach, and in its closer collaboration with the Rudolf Steiner Estate that has taken place recently. What complicates the situation even further is the fact that these 'two souls' often live in the same person. Not a few anthroposophists cultivate the esoteric side of anthroposophy in their private lives, but in their public life they give credit only to the exoteric element—to what the world is ready to accept, above all in the practical fields of work with an anthroposophical background.*

By means of the Christmas Conference of 1923/24, Rudolf Steiner wanted to make his contribution to overcoming this outer and inner divide. A great many of the anthroposophists had placed fields of activity—education, medicine, eurythmy, the threefold social order, the religious life, etc.—fully in the foreground, and allowed anthroposophical truths to recede into the background. Regarding this tendency, Rudolf Steiner writes on 6 July 1924:

* This refers, for example, to Steiner-Waldorf education, biodynamic agriculture and anthroposophical medicine. (Ed.)

> Among the consequences of the Christmas Conference should have been the fact of members [of the Anthroposophical Society] wanting to engage in active work that presents to the world, more and more clearly, what anthroposophy is in its essential being and what it is not. So long as people will go on discussing the fact of whether this or that achievement acquired in the anthroposophical movement ought to be 'slipped' into the conversation without frightening people off by calling it anthroposophy, then many things will continue not to be right within the Anthroposophical Society.
>
> It is a matter of really striving to get clarity in this direction. There is a difference between standing up in a sectarian kind of way for something that has been set up as dogmatic anthroposophy, and the straightforward, open, unvarnished and undisguised standing-up for what anthroposophy gives us in the way of knowledge of the spiritual world, so that human beings can acquire a relationship with this world that is worthy of a human being. (GA 260a, p. 77. *The Constitution of the School of Spiritual Science*)

Many scientists today stand up for what is, for them, the objective truth that there is no objective truth. It does not occur to them at all that their truth, sanctioned and financed by the power of the State, can have the effect of being intolerant and discriminating. This is still a long way from the kind of tolerance where both types of people not only tolerate one another but sincerely respect each other, i.e. those who have the honest conviction that there is no such a thing as objective truth, that in matters of spirit there can only be opinions or subjective faith, and those who are convinced that there is an objective truth a person can grasp, and that a humanity that lives without truth is bound to create indescribable suffering through the egoism which is intrinsic to materialism in the social realm. It holds good for these two types of soul tendencies, too, that they can often live in one and the same person. Many people would like to have an enquiring mind in their private life, but to behave in public as though intellectually materialist science had sole validity.

Mutual respect is made more difficult through the fact that this concerns not only theoretical opinions. Each side sees the other one as socially damaging, as a threat to social peace. The scientists see every seeker of truth as a potential fanatic or as someone who preaches hatred and who wants to exclude anyone who thinks differently. The truth seekers see in every scientist a potential hater of the spirit, hurling humanity deeper and deeper into materialism, where all that remains is 'a war of all against all'. To respect the honest conviction of the other that I am socially damaging (by maintaining my own honest conviction that the other person is socially damaging) would be tolerance indeed. Today's hegemonic scientific sector knows of the possible intolerance and damaging effect of truth seekers, but has no self-knowledge of its own. Rudolf Steiner says, regarding the intolerance of intellectual science:

> I say, fully consciously: Intellectualism is the father of fanaticism, for in no religious institution was there ever to be found such fanaticism as there exists in modern scientific institutions. One just has to know what is pulsating within such tendencies, how far is someone from conceding to the infallibility of the Pope who believes in the invincible infallibility of the professor or even of abstract 'modern science'. The belief in such things is so great because people are absolutely unconscious of the fact that it exists at all, for they take their belief in it for granted. They do not notice any more that in this respect they are stuck in maximum fanaticism.[15] (Lecture of 10 October 1921, GA 343, 1993, p. 608)

Does it not show 'maximum fanaticism' when Professor Clement, at the court of 'academic scholarship', ignores Steiner's founding of the scientific nature of anthroposophy (by referring it to his own perception in the spirit), and publicly denigrates someone who thinks differently from him by calling him, contemptuously, 'paranoid'?

Rudolf Steiner never tired of pointing to the close connection existing between the materialistically abstract intellectualism of science and the social decline of today's humanity. In this book I don't shy away from quoting lengthy passages, as I am convinced that Rudolf Steiner was fully aware, as no one else is—

based on his direct observation of the constellation of spiritual forces—of the true situation of modern humanity. I do not belong to those people who are of the opinion that Steiner is outdated today, and that one must treat the world of science with more tolerance than he himself recommended in his 'overzealous' nature. Words like the following move me most deeply, as I see them come true in today's world:

> If we allow things to run their course as they have been doing, under the influence of the [...] arising world-view [...] then by the end of the twentieth century we shall be facing the war of all against all [...]. We would see a humanity being bred that has no social instincts any more, but would be talking about social matters all the more [...]. The intellectualism that belongs together with materialism has developed humanity to the point that it has brought its intellectual life to the greatest heights [...]. What meanwhile, however, has been raging in their unconscious was the very thing that has enslaved people in their instincts. These must be freed again. But they can only be freed if we [...] from now on have a spiritual world-view that is popularized to the extent that the materialistic world-view has been popularized [...].
>
> For the real result [...] of this intellectualism and materialism of science, the real result altogether of our present attachment to science, is a social life that is chaotic [...].
>
> It is urgently necessary that into our whole life there shall again flow, in a popular way, what speaks of the spiritual world. (See GA 206, pp. 92–3, 105, 111; lectures of 5 and 7 August 1921)

There are people who, due to the fact that they take science seriously, see themselves facing limits. Knowledge of the material world throws up questions for them that can only be answered through a scientific knowledge of the spiritual world. That kind of knowledge cannot be delivered by intellectuality, because it cannot refer them to some perception of spiritual reality. There are people to whom it doesn't occur to believe anything at all of what Steiner says, yet want to assess anthroposophy with their own thinking. They want to find out whether they can understand the world they know better and more profoundly than through the explanations offered by natural science.

There are people who are not convinced by the theory of the 'big bang' or the 'nebular hypothesis', in which there is no mention of any activity on the part of spiritual beings. When Steiner claims to perceive spiritual beings at work during the creation of the world, such people want to examine what he says under the magnifying glass of their thinking. Those are the kind of people who think that the concept of a single human life (as opposed to repeated earth lives by a single human individuality) would be just as absurd as having today without a yesterday or a tomorrow. And when Steiner maintains that he perceives more than a single life for a certain human being, such people are immensely keen on finding out what he has to say.

The only kind of people who can confront the sort of fanaticism that dominates science today are those who, in their search for truth, are able to stand up not with their own fanaticism but courageously and earnestly with a feeling of responsibility for the future of humanity. Time and again Rudolf Steiner deplores the fact that there are so few such people:

> Indeed we must rid ourselves of the prejudice of thinking that it is possible today to convince any of those who are saturated by modern scientific thinking. The elation that some of our short-sighted followers experience again and again, of being able to draw over one or another person, is misplaced. What is important is that people who are free from bias shall be filled with the idea of what anthroposophically orientated spiritual science can give us, and that this modern scientific method should be relentlessly described and characterized to the point where the method itself becomes nonsense, even when it is meant to be benign. We face tremendously earnest times today. Therefore it has to be emphasized, again and again, that as many people as possible who are aware of this seriousness should stand up and not just be prepared to sit down and listen a little, to feel elated by anthroposophical truths, but who want to introduce actively into all aspects of life what anthroposophically orientated spiritual science has to bring, and who also

> have the courage and the strength to stand up for it wherever necessary. Again and again I draw attention to this fact. The battle being waged against spiritual science has taken on all sorts of grotesque, ridiculous, untruthful or even good-natured, but impotent, forms. The battle being waged against this battle is still a very poor one. But it has to be waged for the healing and the further development of humanity. Spiritual science fully appreciates the modern spirit of science where it is justified. Yet, because natural science also wants to be knowledgeable in areas where it understands nothing, it is necessary for healing to take place in whatever materialistic science is making sick. (See GA 206, p. 116 lecture of 7 August 1921)

There is a way forward, if one is prepared to give the spiritual science that exists in today's humanity a chance. This chance depends entirely on the number of human beings who stand up for the truth unreservedly and who want to live by it. Surely no human being can claim to have absolute truth, but every single person who is honest with himself knows whether he strives for the truth unreservedly, or whether he has personal or group interests—however human and understandable they may be—and that these interests can dim his view of the truth and lame his courage for truth.

Rudolf Steiner sees the outstanding truth of our time, as just mentioned, in the necessity of regaining the reality of spirit through scientific knowledge, if humanity is to be rescued from moral decline. Relevant to this is the delivery and flow of Rudolf Steiner's lectures, which are of decisive importance for the effectiveness of anthroposophy within humanity. With the aid of original, unedited manuscripts, which have only very recently been made generally available, it has been demonstrated since 2004 via the publisher Rudolf Steiner Ausgaben that the lectures in the *Gesamtausgabe*[*] are heavily edited. They, too, have been worked on by an intellectual thinking that does not necessarily derive from anthroposophy. According to the director of the Rudolf Steiner Estate:

[*] The Collected Works of Rudolf Steiner in the original German. (Ed.)

> It has become clear, both to me, the Archive director, and also to the board of directors of the Rudolf Steiner Estate that, particularly in the lecture cycles, many passages and whole lectures have been edited to an extent that today would be hardly imaginable. (Letter from David Marc Hoffmann dated 15 April 2013.

This applies not only to 'whole lectures' but to many whole volumes of the *Gesamtausgabe* (GA). Through systematic editing, quite a different spirit often speaks than what one experiences when reading original transcripts. Above all, quite a few inconsistent elements have been introduced into the purity of Steiner's thinking.

A further important truth is that humanity at large represents a single, inseparable organism. It is an illusion to want to promote one's own inner development by disassociating oneself from the rest of humanity. But in order to 'introduce anthroposophy actively into all aspects of life' (p. 57) and in order to represent it publicly, one has to work at one's own thinking in such a way that the necessity of spiritual science for the further development of humanity is convincing. The work on oneself, the deepening of anthroposophy in one's private life or in a small circle of people is essential, particularly in order to find the inner strength to introduce spiritual science into public life, for social destruction through materialistic intellectualism to be prevented. Whoever strives to do this will go through the experience of feeling the kind of outer loneliness[16] that belongs to representing anthroposophy in a world that does not know the reality of spirit. Such a person will always feel themselves to be a beginner.

With regard to humanity as an inseparable unity, the most important thing is to deepen all aspects of the truth regarding the opposing social effect of materialistic science and of spiritual science. With its abstract intellectuality, the world of science has become more and more elite, and the result of this is that it is getting increasingly discriminating and exclusive in a social sense. It creates two classes of people in society: on the one hand, the few very 'clever' ones who can join in this conversation, faithfully followed by the few who would like to keep up with them; and on the other hand, the large number of people who can neither take part in the conversation nor keep up with it. When speaking and writing, we notice among many educated academics a natural disregard for the so-called uneducated people. They seem to think that the fewer the people who understand them the cleverer they are.

The many millions who cannot keep up with the conversation are not permitted to take an active part in public life. All those who do not understand are thrown back into their private life. The power that is wielded over public life lies exclusively in the hands of the scientific sector. As we have seen, a good example of the elite and discriminating attitude of such academics is Christian Clement's Introduction to *SKA*, Volume 5. It is written in a way that the average reader understands nothing—although they would be able to understand it if the person who wrote it had chosen to present even the most complex ideas in a way anyone could understand. Rudolf Steiner wrote that he would like to put his *Philosophy of Freedom* in such a form that it could be read like an exciting novel:

> I would be quite happy if I could shape the form so as to make the content so accessible that philosophical thoughts read like an entertaining and instructive novel. I firmly believe this is possible. (GA 38, p. 19)

Stressing formal perfection is, as has been mentioned, aside from materialism, the other external weapon of intellectuality to exclude so-called ordinary people from science and its power. As an example we can take two imaginary critical editions—let's call them 'A' and 'B'—of Rudolf Steiner's *Philosophy of Freedom*. 'A' is edited according to all the scientific requirements of the academic world, the development of the text documented to the most minute orthographical details and to all fluctuations in punctuation. Edition 'B' is no less scientific than 'A' with regard to all the textual changes that concern the content but, with regard to the orthographic aspect, the punctuation and spelling, it wants to be as approachable as possible by ordinary people.

Because nowadays, to name just one example, a lot of people feel disturbed by the number of old-fashioned grammatical 'dative cases', these have been updated in 'B'.

The publisher of 'B' is of the opinion that edition 'A' should be available, but why should there not be an edition 'B' as well? But the publisher of 'A' sees things quite differently. He is of the opinion that 'B' is unscientific and amateurish. He says that one should not publish such things, there should only be an edition 'A'. And because the publisher of 'A' has the possibility of making himself heard, whereas the publisher of 'B' hasn't, 'A''s publisher can see to it that 'B' is ignored.

In the already mentioned lectures at the East-West Congress in Vienna in 1922, which read like a testament to humanity, Rudolf Steiner, speaking to an audience of 2000 people, points out how important it is today for the preservation of civilization, in order to make society healthy again, that the intellectually educated strata take a serious interest in the new striving for the spirit that shows itself among the supposedly superstitious lower class. A bridge should be built, with the help of which these two classes of people can find one another:

> What is important today is not that we find a way to understand the broad masses, but that we find a way to be understood by the broad masses, that we [...] speak in such a way that we are not felt to be academic, learned, theoretical, but that we are perceived as human beings—felt in such a way that we have something to say that speaks to souls [...] I have never found a hindrance to understanding brought to me from the working class [...]. If we speak out of our whole humanity, then we speak in such a way that the audience has the impression: Something is being said to us here that goes right to our hearts, that has to do with our humanity. Then they see this kind of deeper world-view as the most important thing that can come to them. There is a feeling in the broad masses that enlightenment is the most important thing. [...] People thirst for it, more or less consciously; they thirst for what comes from a real world-view. [...] But if we approach people with a world-view that we take from science, we shall soon be convinced that it is impossible to reach their hearts

> with it, to give people something that touches their humanity. People will always feel that what we offer them in that sense is external to them. If they speak confidentially, they will say to us: What you are saying is all well and good, but we can't understand it, because there are so many things for which we would need to have had a special education. It is not simple enough; it is something that makes us say: One can't follow it. I have heard a lot of people saying that [...]. Whoever looks more closely at what is emerging out of the depths of humanity today, at the kind of human being who is being geared for today's technology, whoever looks into the hearts and souls of these people—who have not gone through a middle school or high school education that attaches so much value to the intellect—will see that in these people there is no inner interest for anything produced by the intellect, but that there is in them something quite different. Something of an elemental nature is revealed here, coming up out of the depths, and which is moving upwards in our social order—something of an elemental nature, which is very little understood in Europe, because it is something new. And when it is understood, it is able to show that we must approach the broad masses with a deeper world-view. [...] We must again be able to speak out of a spirit that moves everybody—from the least to the most educated person. Then we can work together and establish hope in social life in the present and future. (Rudolf Steiner, *Leben im dritten Jahrtausend,* 2nd edn, 2014, pp. 265–86; or GA 83, pp. 254–75, lecture of 10 June, Vienna)

Such reflections make it clear why Rudolf Steiner was so concerned to write his own, exacting *Philosophy of Freedom* in such a way that everybody could understand it. They also show clearly how Steiner speaks to the human being in every person, without differentiating between them.

The key to the way forward in developing spiritual science, not only in private life but also in all realms of life, lies in a new way of looking at the fact that in everybody there lives a human being with an enquiring mind that seeks the truth. Such a way of looking at things cannot happen in a group or an institution; it can only happen in the innermost being of an individual. Every individuality who finds his or her way to the human being within himself—to the human being also within the anthroposophist, to the human being in the member of the Anthroposophical Society or the 'Class'* —will be able to find his way to Anthropos-Sophia, to the wisdom of the human being. For it is not the citizen or the scientist or the anthroposophist who is seeking for anthroposophy, but the human being in the citizen, the human being in the scientist, and the human being in the anthroposophist. That is the future perspective for spiritual science that gives us so much hope: that it is the human being within each person that is searching for it with all his or her strength!

This is also how Rudolf Steiner himself can be freed from the intolerable, unconvincing position of being a 'unique' or 'special case'.[17] The democratic cast of mind of modern humanity demands equality for everyone. The academic world thinks it takes this seriously in that it decrees that there is no such thing as a scientist in spiritual matters, 'special case' or not.

It lies in everyone who so wills to prove with his or her own life that Rudolf Steiner is in no way a unique or a special case, but solely a 'first case'. Each human being is capable of becoming a spiritual scientist in the course of his or her development, just like everyone else. The bourgeois academic establishment sees the equality of all people relating to the fact that nobody can be a spiritual scientist. In the search for free individuality, humanity today is striving for the kind of equality in which everyone has an equal opportunity to become a spiritual scientist.

---

* The First Class of the School of Spiritual Science, based at the Goetheanum in Dornach, Switzerland. (Ed.)

Postscript

In Volume 7 of Professor Clement's *SKA* series—Rudolf Steiner, *Schriften zur Erkenntnisschulung**—his fundamental misjudgement of anthroposophy becomes ever more evident. He writes there:

> According to Steiner, the only being that the human being encounters in meditation is, in the final analysis, his own, which is at the same time individual/personal and universal/absolute.

The appended footnote 14 reads:

> [. . .] If someone were to object that Rudolf Steiner [. . .] has developed a full-fledged theory of angelic hierarchies, he would have to consider that Steiner has also taken these hierarchies back into the human being itself—in accordance with his fundamentally monistic stance: 'He who comes to experience freedom, also finds the hierarchies in the environment of the spiritual human being he then perceives. Then they [the hierarchies] [. . .] are all within the human being, and what is within the human being appears to spiritual vision as his spiritual environment.' (Steiner 1922 in conversation with Walter Johannes Stein [. . .].) (p. xxix)

In such an exposition one can clearly recognize the thinking of Eduard von Hartmann and Kant. Steiner wrote his *Philosophy of Freedom* to overcome such thinking. Clement thinks of human consciousness in terms of a sense-perceptible box, with all possible world contents 'taken into' it. As a consequence, the human being can only acquire knowledge of what falls into this box. Also anthroposophy shows, according to Clement, that there is nothing in it but 'a phenomenology of the contents of human

*Rudolf Steiner, *Schriften—Kritische Ausgabe* (*SKA*), Band 7: *Schriften zur Erkenntnisschulung* (Frommann-Holzboog, November 2014).

consciousness' (p. xxix) — even though 'only one who reads very accurately' would notice that.*

Let's follow through Clement's guiding principle. Let us suppose that two human beings, A and B, think of the folk spirit X, each of them by making it real, 'into the human being itself'. One of the first questions to be asked would be: do A and B take 'into the human being itself' the same contents regarding the folk spirit X, or

---

*Whilst the fifth German edition of this book was in print, a critique of Clement's *SKA* Volume 7 by Ansgar Martins appeared in waldorfblog.wordpress.com. Martins opposes strongly Clement's view that angelic beings exist merely within human consciousness. He writes: 'Clement seems to be unable to accept Steiner's belief in transcendence,' Steiner's 'metaphysical world-view'. Clement's answer to Martins' critique contains the following most telling passage:

> If, according to Steiner's own statement [as made to W.J. Stein], by meeting the spiritual hierarchies in spiritual vision the human being finds nothing else but his own being, is it not legitimate to assume that this is also valid for all other 'beings' which romp about in the 'zoo of anthroposophical beings'? I think one can assume this without contradicting oneself. And if that appears to be solipsism—was not Steiner himself then a solipsist?—On the other hand, if one assumes that Steiner at some time broke with the innermost convictions of his early works and converted to a 'belief' in a transcendence, which is populated with 'beings' existing independently of that being which cognizes and experiences them, I believe one would not be able to substantiate that by quoting Steiner. I'm convinced that such a view would expose Steiner's esotericism to the allegation of being a naive metaphysical realism.

Such words leave no doubt that modern intellectuality can recognize as real only the material world, having no access to spiritual reality. Labelling those who are convinced of the existence of spiritual beings independent of human consciousness as people entertaining a spiritual 'zoo'—where, to mention just one example, the Logos or Christ being also romps about as an animal—strikes a tone that not a few readers might consider blasphemous and hardly attributable to the human spirit. The pages of this Postscript are written with the intent of showing that Anthroposophy, beginning with its basic text *The Philosophy of Freedom*, overcomes the subjective belief in transcendence not by denying the existence of spiritual beings independent of man (which would for instance mean that for the human being A the human being B exists only in his consciousness), but by making all that appears at first to be transcendent to become 'immanent' to intuitive thinking, thanks to a further evolution of thinking itself. (Author's addition to the English translation.)

different ones? If the contents of folk spirit X exist only as 'contents of human consciousness', how can they exist initially outside of such consciousness, in order to be subsequently taken in? And further, is such a folk spirit X taken into human consciousness only once, or repeatedly? Does something remain of such a folk spirit X that exists outside of the human beings A and B—and if so, what kind of existence does it have? Another no less important question is: what can A take into his own being of the contents of B's consciousness, and B of the contents of A's consciousness?

In trying to give a detailed answer to the above questions one becomes aware of the contrast between the two thinkers Hartmann and Steiner. In the first Appendix to his *Philosophy of Freedom* Rudolf Steiner summarizes such a problem in the following way:

> [...] there are thinkers who [...] say: my conscious world is enclosed within me; in the same way, any other conscious world is enclosed within itself. I cannot see into the world of consciousness of another person. How, then, do I know that he and I are both in the same world? The theory which believes it possible to infer from the conscious world an unconscious world [...] says: the world I have in my consciousness is the representative in me of a real world to which I have no conscious access. In this real world lie the unknown causes of my conscious world. [...] It is clear that to the world accessible to my consciousness an inaccessible one is here being added hypothetically, since one believes that otherwise one is forced to the conclusion that the whole external world, which I think is there in front of me, is nothing but the world of my consciousness, and to the further—solipsistic—absurdity that other people, too, exist only within my consciousness.

The fundamental essence of the evolution of consciousness, as developed through spiritual science, can be seen in the dialogue between two people described in the aforementioned first Appendix to *The Philosophy of Freedom*. Rudolf Steiner describes the phenomenon as follows. What I see as an outer expression of the other person, and what I hear him communicating to me out of his interior world,

> [. . .] sets my thinking activity in motion. Through the thinking with which I confront the other person, the percept of him becomes, as it were, transparent to the mind. I am bound to admit that when I grasp the percept with my thinking, it is not at all the same thing as appeared to the outer senses. In what is a direct appearance to the senses, something else is indirectly revealed. The mere sense appearance extinguishes itself at the same time as it confronts me. But what it reveals through this extinguishing compels me as a thinking being to extinguish my own thinking as long as I am under its influence, and to put *its* thinking in place of mine. I then grasp *its* thinking in my thinking as an experience like my own. I have really perceived another person's thinking. [. . .] this is a process lying wholly *within* my consciousness and consisting in this, that the other person's thinking takes the place of mine. Through the self-extinction of the sense appearance, the separation between the two spheres of consciousness is actually overcome. This expresses itself in my consciousness through the fact that while experiencing the content of another person's consciousness I experience my own consciousness as little as I experience it in dreamless sleep.*

Rudolf Steiner goes on to describe that what happens is a swift to-and-fro between waking up in the intuitive thinking of the other person—while one's own consciousness falls asleep, just as happens in dreamless sleeping—and waking up again within the content of one's own thinking.

---

*These quotations are taken from the first Appendix to the 1918 (second) edition of *The Philosophy of Freedom*. In a recent article by Christian Clement, published in *Das Goetheanum* and entitled 'Diese Freiheit stirbt nicht im Kugelhagel'—'This Freedom Does Not Die in a Hail of Bullets' (16 January 2015, p. 3), the author sees an affinity to the spirit of freedom of the Paris cartoonists from the magazine *Charlie Hebdo* in Rudolf Steiner's *Philosophy of Freedom*, '. . . especially in its earlier version of 1894'. The subtitle of the article runs: 'Rudolf Steiner was also "Charlie"'. Clement's preference for the 1894 edition seems to imply that Steiner later on broke with the original spirit of his *Philosophy of Freedom*, in which there was no reference to spiritual beings that exist and act independently of human consciousness. But in both editions Steiner remains true to himself by seeing intuitive thinking as the free spiritual activity through which the human spirit overcomes the sphere of consciousness bestowed on him by nature. (Author's addition to the English edition.)

In his explanations Clement knows only the two possibilities of something being either within or without. He is right in rejecting as self-deception all that is considered as being outside, as being beyond or transcendent. But no reality that is experienced as being beyond can be transformed offhand into something that is within, into a 'content of human consciousness.' To that purpose, it is necessary to submit consciousness itself to a *substantial change*. One has to become able to see (Imagination) and hear (Inspiration) in the spiritual realm through a further evolution of thinking. The next-following step is to penetrate both Imagination and Inspiration with intuitive thinking, in the same way that we penetrate sense perception with thinking.

The problem of the beyond, therefore, lies not in the fact that something is beyond my consciousness, as if it were on the other side of it. To the contrary, the problem lies in the fact that I myself remain *on this side* with my consciousness. I will only be able to step out of my being, trapped on this side, on my own side, by overcoming that separation which is due to my undeveloped consciousness. The world doesn't have to stop being beyond my consciousness. Much to the contrary, rather, it is I myself who must stop remaining within my own consciousness on this side of the world. I have to transform my own state of consciousness. This cannot happen by stuffing all kinds of world contents into my unchanged consciousness. It can only happen if I *transform it thoroughly,* and this can only be achieved through a further evolution of thinking.

And what happens in the case of a 'dialogue' between a human spirit and folk spirit X that we were just talking about? Also, in the case of a body-free spirit is it necessary for human thinking to delete the aspect of perception? All that is perceived as being outside must become 'transparent to the mind'. In all that I see (Imagination) and hear (Inspiration) of folk spirit X—not with bodily but with soul perception—in this twofold inner perception, in 'what is a direct appearance to the [inner] senses, something else is indirectly revealed.' Through thinking intuition, 'the separation between the two spheres of consciousness'—the sphere of consciousness of folk spirit X and that of the human being—'is actually overcome'. What happens is not, as Clement maintains, that folk spirit X is 'taken [...] back into the human being itself', but rather the very opposite. The sphere of consciousness of the human being 'is actually overcome' through waking up into the thinking activity of folk spirit X. This does not mean that the human being intuitively makes *all* thinking contents of folk spirit X his own. In such a case he himself would be that spirit.

But Rudolf Steiner never tired of emphasizing that such intuitive, objectively scientific knowledge of something spiritual can only be obtained by someone who has brought all Imagination and Inspiration to the point of being 'extinguished'. The organs of bodily sense perception are given to us by nature; the organs of soul perception can only be unfolded through the further evolution of thinking. By using bodily sense perception we create, through thinking, a 'natural science'; by using soul sense perception we create, through that very same thinking, a 'spiritual science', which is no less objective and factual than natural science.

Nowhere is a reference to such a spiritual science found in Clement's commentaries, neither in his 5th nor in his 7th volume. Nowhere does he recognize the reality of spirit, with its faculty of intuitive thinking. This total lack is evidenced, for instance, where he writes that through 'spirit' we simply 'add a spiritual dimension' (p. lxxxviii) to our understanding of soul. He even speaks of what is '"spiritual" as a dimension of the inner life of the human being which has been overlooked and forgotten' (ibid.). In all his discussions one finds only a self-contained human consciousness. All world contents are contemplated only in so far as they are 'taken back into' human consciousness. Spiritual science considers all of that as belonging to 'soul'. The human being becomes 'spirit' only through spiritualizing what consists of soul, which happens through an ongoing dissolution of boundaries. Day-to-day consciousness has to be expanded to the point of comprehending all beings and processes of the world in an intuitively thinking way. By becoming an intuitively thinking spirit, one leaves all 'inner life' of the soul behind oneself.

Everything spiritual is beyond space and time. With respect to spirit it makes no sense to speak of being inside or outside. Also, in the dialogue with W.J. Stein that Clement refers to, Steiner speaks of a 'spiritual environment'. A *spiritual* environment has nothing to do with space. If that were the case, Steiner would be contradicting himself in using two mutually exclusive wordings, as he speaks of 'what is within the human being' on the one hand and what is 'his spiritual environment'—outside of him—on the other hand. The concept of a 'spiritual environment' can be seen as akin to the concept of a 'spiritual affinity'. The physical or blood affinity of a person has to do with space, but the *spiritual* affinity is like a spiritual environment in which space plays no role.

One of the numerous consequences of Professor Clement's failure to recognize the reality of spirit is found in his statement that Steiner's treatment of psychoanalysis 'can only be characterized as being superficial' (p. xxxv). Thus, Clement invents a soul quality in relation to Steiner, and then overlooks the fact that Steiner only sought to make statements about psychoanalysis that are *spiritually scientific,* meaning that they are factual and objective. When Goethe fought against Newton's *Opticks,* he did not intend to say that Newton's ideas are 'superficial'—such a statement may be made by moralizers—but as a natural scientist Goethe wanted to prove factually that Newton's ideas are mistaken. Science has to do with right and wrong in relation to facts, which Clement calls 'factual distance from the object' (see p. 24), and not with superficiality or profoundness, which are moral qualities of persons.

To mention one concrete fact pointed out by Steiner concerning psychoanalysis: the physiology upon which psychoanalysis rests is called amateurish by Steiner. He called it 'dilettantish' because the physiologist who lacks anthroposophy does not know of the action of cosmic ether in building the physical organism (see for instance the lecture of 20 July 1923, where Steiner in addition to 'dilettantish' also uses the words 'incomplete' and 'defective'). Professor Clement could try to prove that Steiner's statements on the function of cosmic ether contradict other ascertained facts, and that they are therefore wrong or amateurish—but as a scientist he cannot call them superficial. Incidentally, in calling Steiner 'superficial' why doesn't Clement give any reference to the 'profundity' (that he must be aware of) through which it becomes obvious that Steiner's treatment of psychoanalysis 'can only be characterized as being superficial'? Why, as a scientist, does he expect that his reader should simply believe him?

Here let me briefly quote another example of spiritual research which claims to be factually objective and scientific. As a result of his spiritual research, Rudolf Steiner states that the leaders of sects in the West are superhuman beings with the task of working against anthroposophy (see p. 74). I ask Professor Clement the question as to whether he finds such a statement to be superficial. Does it also simply represent a 'dimension of the inner life' of Rudolf Steiner? How is it possible for him to repeatedly look into Steiner's inner life with the conviction that he understands it better than Steiner himself?

The moralizing accusation of being superficial tallies with the already mentioned, no less moralizing accusation of being immature. Professor Clement sees in the author of the Mystery Dramas 'an unarguable lack of dramatic and artistic maturity' (see p. 41). Clement cannot reasonably state that Steiner was immature only in writing his Mystery Dramas, but that he was a mature person in writing his other works. He cannot reasonably hold that Steiner was superficial solely in his assessment of psychoanalysis, while in other matters he showed profound depth. No one can be immature and superficial in some areas whilst being mature and profound in others, just as no one can be stupid in some areas and very intelligent in others. Stupidity remains stupidity—and superficiality remains superficiality. As far as maturity is concerned, one can, of course, be immature in one's early years and ripen in the course of time. But according to Clement, the 53-year-old Steiner, who by 1914 had finished writing his four Mystery Dramas, was still immature. This means that Steiner was no less immature in 1909 when he finished writing his *Occult Science – An Outline.* But even when Clement discusses the lectures Steiner gave in 1924 (see pp. 40–41), shortly before his death, he offers no indication that the 64-year-old Steiner had become more mature. He maintains that Steiner was still 'interpreting' in the old manner. To the very end there is no mention of a scientific knowledge of spiritual matters.

Thus, the reader is confronted with an editor of Rudolf Steiner's works who deems Rudolf Steiner to be superficial and immature. I have endeavoured to show in this book that, in his dealing with anthroposophy, Clement nowhere reaches the level of enquiry proper to spiritual science. He treats Rudolf Steiner's texts as philosophical or literary products which have no claim to be treatises of spiritual science. He deals with them from the point of view of an implied, unavowed dogma that a *science of spirit* is an impossibility.

Such a manner of dealing with anthroposophy is amateurish in two respects. It is amateurish not only due to the fact that it treats Rudolf Steiner's spiritual science as the product of a superficial and immature person, but even more so because Clement's basic assumption, or hypothesis, which decrees that there is no such thing as a science of spirit, is nowhere uttered or articulated. To say this says nothing about the person Christian Clement; rather, it points to the fact that his treatment of anthroposophy can in no way be considered to be scientific.

The review *Das Goetheanum* (28 November 2014, pp. 5-7: 'Rudolf Steiner Interessant Machen'—'Making Rudolf Steiner Interesting') gives Christian Clement, professor at a Mormon university, the opportunity of presenting himself over three pages. A box text on p. 6 brings out the essence of his discourse:

> Steiner's theory of clairvoyance is a position that ought to be considered in scientific discourse.

Translated into plain language that means: Steiner has put forward no more than a 'theory', a system of ideas, concerning 'clairvoyance'. He has made no actual researches in the spiritual realms through perception and thinking; there exist no factual findings of spiritual investigation. But Steiner's 'position' or theory deserves to be scrutinized all the same by academia, because its scientists have all the prerequisites that enable them to verify 'Steiner's spiritually-scientific hypotheses' (p. 6).

If *Das Goetheanum*, the official journal of the Anthroposophical Society, would also give a platform to voices that are critical of Clement, one would be able to say that it is a magazine where a fair exchange of opinions takes place—where one can read positions and counter-positions.* Why shouldn't Professor Clement's work be subject to that standard? But that is not the case. Since the publication of Volume 5 of *SKA* in August 2013, no critical opinion of Clement's work has been published in *Das Goetheanum.*

On the first page of the aforementioned article is a photo of Clement—surrounded by text which creates a kind of halo. The whole presentation might lead the reader to say to himself: Isn't it obvious that leading members of the Anthroposophical Society are glad about the fact that the weight of an academic scientist—a professor at a Mormon university in the USA—edits works of Rudolf Steiner and publishes them with an academic publisher? Is this not a welcome way of freeing anthroposophy from all fanaticism and dilettantism which discredits it? Isn't it a way of 'Making Rudolf Steiner Interesting'?

At the same time that Clement's interview was featured in *Das Goetheanum*, a pocket book appeared from the independent publisher Rudolf Steiner Ausgaben bearing the title: Rudolf Steiner, *Gibt es eine Geistes*wissenschaft? ('Is There Such a Thing as a *Science* of the Spirit?', lectures of 22, 23 and 24 October 1920,

---

*The author is here referring to articles and features. As of January 2015, several reader's letters critical of *SKA* and Christian Clement's approach have been published in *Das Goetheanum.*

not translated, GA 200). In this book there is no talk of 'Steiner's theory of clairvoyance' or of 'Steiner's spiritually-scientific hypotheses'. Instead, the reader finds a Rudolf Steiner who speaks for himself. Over many pages, Rudolf Steiner describes what he perceives, and penetrates with thinking, concerning the leading figures in the known sects of the West, to which also the Mormons belong. He says that certain spiritual beings have the task of opposing anthroposophy, which can only cause endless destruction and suffering throughout the world. Rudolf Steiner speaks of a spiritual battle and deplores that there are so few people aligning themselves on the side of spiritual beings that foster the good in the evolution of man. He says:

> But how difficult it is for spiritual science and for a spiritually-scientific culture in its struggle to establish itself, a culture that is not simply wanted but is a necessity. Everywhere we find at work those who want to prevent this spiritual science from establishing itself. We have very few dynamic workers on the side of spiritual science, whereas those who work destructively show themselves full of energy. (p. 124)
>
> The enemies, my dear friends, are standing guard. The enemies are waging a fierce battle. Our fighting, all that we are able to do, is feeble, very feeble, and our understanding of anthroposophy is in many respects drowsy, really drowsy. Therein lies the profound suffering experienced by whoever becomes fully aware of the present situation. (p. 162)

Such words make it clear that everyone siding with anthroposophy, everyone wanting to dedicate his life to spiritual science, has to know that earthly power aligns with the other side. He or she will have to accept that such a power will label him an amateur, a fanatic or something similar. Steiner's words quoted above make it clear that he felt quite alone in this world with his spiritual science. But he knew that he had all good spiritual beings on his side, and this was good enough for him.

Notes

1. Goethe's Collected Works, Part 33, National Scientific Works, Volume 1, edited by Rudolf Steiner, Berlin and Stuttgart (1883), 'Happy Event', p. 112.
2. Rudolf Steiner, 'Mysticism at the Dawn of the Modern Age of Spiritual Life and its Relationship to the Modern World-view' (1901); Rudolf Steiner, 'Christianity as Mystical Fact and the Mysteries of Antiquity' (1902). Respective English editions: *Mystics After Modernism*, SteinerBooks, 2003 (GA 7); *Christianity as Mystical Fact and the Mysteries of Antiquity*, RSP, 2000 (GA 8).
3. I speak solely in the sense of the objective fact of a wrong portrayal, without any reference to personal intention.
4. Quotations from lectures in the GA are based on the 'cleartext' transcript (www.steiner-klartext.net).
5. For a deepening of the relationship between percept, idea, memory and Imagination see, for example, Rudolf Steiner's letter to members of the Anthroposophic Society, 'Man's Freedom and the Michael Age' (GA 26, pp. 213–18), which appears as Chapter XXII in *The Michael Mystery*, Anthroposophic Press 1956.
6. Even Clement's rendering of Rudolf Steiner's 'highly complex ideas' contains a series of coarse distortions. All three of Clement's main statements about 'the Jesus who bore the Christ Being', which applies from his 30th till his 33rd year, are wrong:

   a) His astral body is *not* that of the 'earlier Buddha'. When the Luke-Jesus, in his 12th year, discards the astral mother sheath, the Buddha becomes one with this sheath *in the spiritual world* (GA 114, p. 73. *According to Luke*, lecture of 17 September 1909, Basel, SteinerBooks, 2001).

   b) In the Luke-Jesus, the sister soul of Adam, which had remained paradisaical, was incarnated for the first time. The Luke-Jesus, even as the Christ bearer, has *nothing* within himself of the Adam soul who descended into the earthly stream of repeated incarnations.

c) During the whole of the three years, Zarathustra's I *did not* inhabit Jesus at all. In his 30th year, before the entry of the Christ, he departed from the three bodies of Jesus.

Clement's statement about the two Jesus boys before the 30th year is also wrong. There was *no* 'mutual exchange of bodily elements'. In the 12th year of his life, the ego of Zarathustra, who up till then had lived in the Matthew Jesus, enters the Luke Jesus who, up until then, had no ego.

7. Also with regard to Steiner's Mystery Dramas, Clement writes that Steiner has again speculatively 'postulated' their contents (see quotation on p. 38).
8. In an essay in the *Archivemagazine*, Contributions to Rudolf Steiner's Complete Works (December 2013)—'The Basis of the Philosophical Consciousness of Anthroposophy: Rudolf Steiner's Books on "Mysticism" and "Christianity" in a Critical Light'—Clements writes:

> p. 178, footnote 5: 'The way in which the Being that is conceived of in those conceptions can also be cognized in a non-representative, non-projective form, plays a merely subordinate role in the books of 1901 and 1902 and is the actual theme of Steiner's texts about the school of knowledge.'
> pp. 187–8, footnote 15: 'According to Steiner this being itself can certainly enter into our knowledge, but first of all the conceptual character of consciousness as such has to be overcome (see the works presented in SKA 7 on the training in knowledge).'

The 'conceptual character of consciousness as such' must, according to Clement, be overcome if the spiritual nature of being has to 'enter into our knowledge'. According to Steiner, it is not the 'conceptual character' that has to be overcome in knowing spiritual being but, entirely to the contrary, the *imaginative content* of consciousness. The content of a mental picture is something that is given in normal consciousness. The imaginative content can, to the contrary, only be produced actively by way of the *further development of thinking*. It arises through an *intensification of the thinking activity itself*, as a beginning in overcoming one's passive beholding of what is outside, as experienced in sense perception and ordinary thinking. It is the beginning in overcoming every representation of a 'distance' or duality of subject and object. In that Clement does not recognize this beginning, this first necessary step to a spiritually intuitive union in thought, he speaks about something 'entering into our knowledge'. The picture of a spatial 'entering into' something is in no way accidental. It is an idea that is formed according to *sense perception*. It is similar to what E. v. Hartmann wrote in connection to the *The Philosophy of Freedom*: 'One's consciousness cannot look into that of someone else's [...].' To which Steiner writes: 'One's consciousness cannot look into that of someone else's—this is the coarsest form of naive realism. This is imagined entirely according to the analogy of material processes.' (See Rudolf Steiner, *The Philosophy of Freedom*, Bad Liebenzell, 2nd edn, 2013, p. 357.) Thus Clement remains, to the end, caught up in intellectuality that pictures the relationship between man and the world as being like a naively realistic, sense-perceptible to-ing and fro-ing. (See also the spatial idea of 'behind' on p. 80.)

This is where the basic misjudgement of Rudolf Steiner's spiritual science lies on the part of the *intellectuality* that we are talking about in this book. The content of Steiner's *Christianity* is not the result of forming mental pictures or ideas—nor the merely imagined overcoming of the 'idea character of consciousness as such'—but of the further development of thinking. Clement treats this kind of content as though it were not the imaginative side of spiritual Being grasped by intuitive thinking, but the result of the kind of forming of ideas that is at work *before* a further development of thinking takes place—i.e. as though it were to maintain a subjective and personal character—whilst for Steiner it belongs to the scientific knowledge of spirit that is based on objective truth.

9. To give an example, when Clement presented them with his dissertation on Steiner's Mystery Dramas on the occasion of attaining his doctorate, they would feel elated in reading the following. (On the left-hand side there is the text that was officially submitted in 2005, and on the right-hand side the significant revision for the book version of 2007.)

	'[Quotation from: Rudolf Steiner's *Wahrspruchworte*, p. 224 (In Clement's version the italics are missing and the semicolon is replaced by a full stop.):]
'So although Steiner's philosophical writings between 1882 and 1897 were mainly exercises in "the grammar of knowledge" there always stood behind them similar "dramatic" inner experiences and battles, as described in the apocalyptic literature and the Mystery Dramas.	'One should not want to give up the knowledge drama in favour of a knowledge grammar; nor even *fear* may keep us from falling into the abyss of individualism, for we arise from this abyss accompanied by many spirits, and experiences oneself related to them [...]'.
'Steiner's personal "knowledge drama" leads him from an uncritical admiration of Goethe during the 80s to a radical individualism and anarchy in the 90s, in which his "ego" as it were blew up to absolute proportions.	'Steiner's own "knowledge drama" then also leads him into the "abyss of individualism", namely from the uncritical admiration of Goethe during the 80s to a radical individualism and anarchy during the 90s, in which his "ego" as it were blew up to absolute proportions.
'At the turn of the century there then followed a turn to mysticism and theosophy, in the course of which Steiner as it were gave up his previous "ego" and changed from being a radical individualist to being a theosophist bound to dogmas and hierarchies.	'At the turn of the century there then followed a turn to mysticism and theosophy, in the course of which Steiner as it were gave up his previous "ego" and changed from being a radical individualist to being a theosophist bound to dogmas and official duties.
'However out of this "sacrifice" Steiner the anthroposophist was born.'	'However out of this "sacrifice" Steiner the anthroposophist was born.'
(*The Birth of the Modern Mystery Dramas out of the Spirit of Weimar.* Text of the original dissertation of 2005, p. 23, website: byu.academia.edu/Christian Clement)	(*The Birth of the Modern Mystery Dramas out of the Spirit of Weimar*, Logos Publications, Berlin 2007, p. 21)

I just want to say this much about the above revision: in the version that was handed in to the Mormon university in 2005, Steiner's quote dismissing any kind of 'grammar of knowledge' is missing. Steiner is of the opinion that it is not sufficient merely to think out a *theory* of knowledge intellectually—that is what he means by '*grammar* of knowledge'. A human being must go through an inner transformation, he must experience an inner '*drama* of knowledge' through further development of thinking. According to Steiner, a human being experiences multiple self-overcomings on the three levels of knowledge of spirit as a result of inner battles. But in the version Clement handed in, he maintains that up till 1897 Steiner had essentially been doing 'exercises in grammar of knowledge'—and that the drama part of it had only been done *behind* this (where? see also the talk about 'entering into' p. 80). This should also apply to *The Philosophy of Freedom*, which appeared in 1894, about which Steiner writes the following:

> I shall tell you about the way I experienced it. Everything in my book is meant personally. [...] You can do nothing for anyone who wants to go along with you over rocks and abysses. You must find your own way of getting over them [...] Arbitrarily, in an absolutely individual way, I jumped over many a rock and worked my way through thickets entirely in my own fashion. [...] I am hardly interested in philosophy anymore, except for it being my own individual experience. (Letter to Rosa Mayreder on 4 November 1894)

Steiner's inclusion in the 'hierarchies' of the theosophists, too, must appeal more readily to the Mormon hierarchy than the 'office duties' that were used later on for the general public.

Any elder among the Mormons who read the version submitted in 2005 had every reason to not only employ Clement as a professor in their university, but also to support financially his publication of the works of Rudolf Steiner. (See *SKA* Volume 5, p. iv)

10. In the original version of his dissertation, as presented in May 2005 when receiving his doctorate from the University of Utah, the second part of the quotation runs as follows:

> In that we can describe Imagination in the terminology of *The Philosophy of Freedom* as the inner view of those soul/spiritual processes that lead to idea-forming becoming condensed into pictures, the continuity of

> Steiner's thinking becomes evident. (p. 69, see website byu.academia.edu/ChristianClement)

It has been explained in the first part of this book that, according to Steiner, the inner process that leads to Imagination is quite different from the 'soul/spiritual processes that lead to forming mental pictures'. Clement's presentation of the source of anthroposophy is intrinsically wrong. Therein lies the lack of a scientific basis that, according to Clement's Introduction, is given only through 'due distance to the object' (p. xxxi).

11. 'Outgrowth' is the literal translation of the German *Auswuchs* which, according to Duden, has a negative meaning. But Clement himself uses this word in a neutral/positive sense—as in the *Archivemagazine*, December 2013, p. 181.
12. The English 'abstruse' means, in addition to abstruse, also puzzling, highly complex, confused. Someone who has German as their mother tongue sensibly chooses the English 'abstruse' in so far as it corresponds to the German 'abstruse'.
13. As an example of this, one can mention *Irreducible Mind, Towards a Psychology for the 21st Century* by Edward F. Kelly among others (Rowman & Littlefield Publishers, 2009). It is a passionate refutation of the widespread conviction that one can explain all the aspects of the human mind 'as brain activity'. Despite this, the name of Rudolf Steiner does not occur anywhere throughout the book's 800 pages (among which are 150 pages of references and indexes). A further example comes from the philosopher Hartmut Traub, who reproaches Clement in regard to 'European Spiritual History', of pursuing an 'anthroposophical instrumentalizing' (p. 22), in which anthroposophy itself runs the risk of suffering a '*spiritual loss of substance*' (p. 21). (See 'Welten, die sie trennen!', www.academia.edu/7346033/.)
14. In the weekly journal *Das Goetheanum*, the official organ of the Anthroposophical Society, Johannes Kiersch defends Christian Clement in an essay entitled 'Warum nicht miteinander redden?'—'Why not speak with one another?' (6 June 2014, p. 10-11). He vehemently opposes '... the odd phenomenon of excitement at the appearance of the new "critical edition" [of Clement's] that to begin with had such an absurd effect ...' (p. 11). With such words he announces his readiness to speak with those people who think

differently from him, by summoning them to speak together ('why not speak with one another?'). However, the Anthroposophical Society as the publisher of *Das Goetheanum* does not allow the people who are regarding Clement critically to have any say. The reader is not permitted to have any direct perception of the convictions that are being labelled as 'absolutely absurd' in the official weekly. There is no answer to his question: Why not speak to one another in *Das Goetheanum* too.*

15. The claim to power 'of the abstract agency named "modern science"' is sealed through its amalgamation with the power of the State. The reader who holds the opinion that Steiner is exaggerating when he talks about a 'maximum fanaticism' needs only read the response to the first edition of this book that Professor Clement uploaded to the internet. Here is an excerpt:

    > [...] there enters with Pietro Archiati a further religious fighter into the lists, tangled up in paranoid pictures of the enemy and attacking the critical Steiner edition [...] The first part pretends to be a discussion of the contents, but in part two and three we see that the introduction to *SKA* does not present Archiati with a new interpretation of Steiner that would invite making a critical argument, but rather a crusade against Steiner and anthroposophy that he can meet only with defence reflexes. In his passionate plea for a strict anthroposophical isolationism [...] he does not discuss Clement himself, but a scarecrow hammered together out of two classical pictures of the enemy [...]. (Quoted in: *Symptomatologische Illustrationen*, Forum, February–March 2014, p. 3, stating the following source: http://www.academia.edu/5553990/)

    Apart from everything else, it can shock one to see with what human contempt a professor at a Mormon university in the USA can express himself via the internet, in the eyes of the whole world—through which people who think differently are reduced, among other things, to being 'paranoid', and 'religious fighters' who react like unreasoning animals, 'only with defence reflexes'.

16. May a reference to my own destiny be allowed here. A previous Chairman of the Anthroposophical Society wrote, among other things, that my convictions 'do damage to the Anthroposophical

*In, *Anthroposophy Worldwide*, the twin review of *Das Goetheanum*, the voices critical of Christian Clement do also have their say. (Ed.)

Society rather than edifying it' (*Das Goetheanum, Mitteilungen* 23 February 1997, p. 283). At that time, and up until today, no single voice had the insight and courage to speak up and say that when a person with power labels a person who has a different opinion to be 'damaging' due to his views, without giving that person a chance to make a statement to his readers about this condemnation, that is not only an expression of opinion that has no further consequences, but is an exercise of power that effectively ostracizes the condemned person. All the office holders and group leaders who want to remain 'faithful' to the leadership of their Society, or want to further enjoy its favours, will find it impossible to invite as a speaker or recommend the books of such a person who has been put in the pillory. And until today I hear people saying that I left the Anthroposophical Society entirely voluntarily, have not overcome my personal hurt, and am an embittered enemy of the Anthroposophical Society. Over the years, I have often thought of the people in Germany whose work was declared to be 'degenerate' in the period leading up to the last World War.

17. It seems to me that Rudolf Steiner presents human *thinking* with a special challenge. Whoever reads Steiner's books and lectures is confronted with a spiritual science that portrays a quite new step in the development of human consciousness—a step which is not achieved gradually and through the contributions of many people, but in a single stroke and by a single person. Over the years, I have come increasingly to the following thoughts, which I would like to present in the form of a working hypothesis to those readers who have an interest. The Logos Spirit, the cosmic wisdom of love as an all-encompassing spiritual Being, has connected itself with a human being, as an archetypal phenomenon, two times—the first time in a body/soul union, the second time in a soul/spirit union. The first time was about 2000 years ago, and was to give to all human beings the inner capacity of freedom, for to love human beings means to enable them to be free. The second time, about 100 years ago, was to enable every human being to perceive the archetypal phenomenon of the actual exercising of freedom. Exercising freedom means to live as an intuitive thinking and free willing spirit in a world of spirits. In Rudolf Steiner's anthroposophy this archetypal phenomenon becomes perceptible to

everyone. That this came about through one single person (Rudolf Steiner) is not so much due to this person himself, but much more to the 'return'—to the second coming of the Logos Spirit. Thus, the doors are opened to untruth when, in Rudolf Steiner's lectures, 'we' is changed to 'you', in which case the speaker is being placed outside the human realm. I quote just one example among the countless ones available (additions in square brackets are from myself):

> Here you [we] acquire a certain view of things. Here you [we] get the point of view that your [our] moral soul attitude is continually being answered from out of the spiritual world. You [we] take what the spiritual world is forming in you [us] into your [our] physical and your [our] etheric existence. In doing this you [we] are bringing in the voice of conscience. In waking life what you [we] get as an answer shapes itself into forms and colouring, into the voice of conscience. Altogether all that makes up our [!] inner moral mood we [!] must relate out of this sort of knowledge to the condition of sleep. (GA 208, p. 186, *Cosmosophy*, Vol. 2)

Like everyone else, Rudolf Steiner in his future earth lives will also be faced with the task of making through the individual exercise of freedom out of anthroposophy as becoming conscious of the possible transformation of man—*Anthroposophy as making such transformation real*—a transformation for which the whole of earth evolution will be needed. The beginning of such a transformation lies in a further development of thinking, to which a whole life can be devoted, and which can be achieved best of all through the study of spiritual science—above all *The Philosophy of Freedom* by Rudolf Steiner.

Select Bibliography

Works by Rudolf Steiner in English Translation

RSP:	Rudolf Steiner Press, London/Forest Row, East Sussex
AP/SB:	SteinerBooks, Great Barrington, MA

GA 4	*The Philosophy of Freedom*, RSP, 2011
GA 7	*Mystics after Modernism*, SB 2003/*Mysticism at the Dawn of the Modern Age*, Blaufelt, NY, 1980
GA 8	*Christianity as Mystical Fact and the Mysteries of Antiquity*, RSP 2000/SB 2006
GA 13	*Occult Science – An Outline*, RSP, 2005/*An Outline of Esoteric Science*, SB 1998
GA 14	*Four Mystery Plays*, SB 2007
GA 26	*The Michael Mystery*, AP 1956/*Anthroposophical Leading Thoughts: Anthroposophy as a Path of Knowledge – The Michael Mystery*, RSP 1998
GA 27	Rudolf Steiner and Ita Wegman, *Extending Practical Medicine*, RSP, London 2000
GA 28	*Autobiography*, SB 2006
GA 83	*The Tension between East and West*, SB 2000
GA 114	*According to Luke*, SB 2001
GA 205	*Therapeutic Insights: Earthly and Cosmic Laws*, Mercury Press, 1984
GA 207	*Cosmosophy*, Vol. 1, AP, 1985
GA 208	*Cosmosophy*, Vol. 2, Completion Press, Gympie, Australia, 1997
GA 236	*Karmic Relationships: Esoteric Studies*, Vol. II, RSP 2004
GA 260a	*The Constitution of the School of Spiritual Science*, RSP 1980
GA 332a	*The Social Future*, RSP 2013